Second Chances

SECOND CHANCES

POETRY FROM A

Sun-Kissed Life

AYALA ZARFJIAN

2019
GOLDEN DRAGONFLY PRESS

FIRST PRINT EDITION, May 2019
FIRST EBOOK EDITION, May 2019

ISBN: 978-1-7325772-9-9
ISBN: 1-7325772-9-3

Library of Congress Control Number: 2019940649

Printed on acid-free paper supplied by a Forest Stewardship Council-certified
provider. Cream paper is made from 30% post-consumer waste recycled material.

First published in the United States of America
by Golden Dragonfly Press, 2019.

www.goldendragonflypress.com

For the boys that reside in my soul, Carl, Joshua, Daniel, and Aiden.

For mom and dad for loving me unconditionally.

For grandpa Yancu. He walked a thousand stairs to feed my belly and my soul.

For my first editor Daniel.

Contents

"I can hear my bones straining under the weight of all of the lives I'm not living."

—Jonathan Safran Foer

The Places You Will Go

For Aiden

The storm rolled in,
the trees were stark,
against the dark sapphire sky,
the roads an endless white blanket.
How quiet it gets
when it snows,
I thought the day you were born.
Love was held in each breath,
in your eyes I discovered
the constellations
of the sky.
I cradled you in my arms,
my heart racing.
I wanted to live,
to love you
through your first scraped knees,
watch over you when you climb trees,
read you bedtime stories.
I wanted to live
to watch your pearly teeth
sprout like limbs of a young tree.
I wanted to guide you to catch
your first fish,
while the seagulls watch in anticipation waiting to steal it.
I wanted to hear about your first kiss,
when your lips feel like they're on fire,
when they feel soft like billowy clouds.
I wanted to build bridges between
your generation and mine.
Share postcards of oceans I have crossed,
of places you will go one day,
when you grow up to be a man.

1

Building your own life,
your own future.
I wanted to play games
I had played with my brothers,
when we were children,
build forts out of sheets and pillows.
I wanted to dance with you in the kitchen,
the way I dance with your grandfather
when the harvest moon floats in the sky.
I wanted,
I wanted,
I want
your breath to be yours,
your space to be free,
your journey to be one of discovery.
Shape your world,
and mold it with your interpretation and your intention.
Navigate your compass with true wisdom,
questioning,
seeking,
loving.

A New World

My father
created a life
out of thin air.
He built a foundation
with his strong hands,
and his strong mind.
He built a home,
raised a family,
and found success.
He uprooted
to a new land,
to plant new trees,
on a new landscape,
on a blank canvas,
for his sons and daughter.
He left notoriety,
a good name,
a reputation,
to start over.
He became invisible,
suffered tragedies and challenges in his new world,
for all of us to find peace
from the impending war.
He sacrificed himself for the country,
but he did not want to
sacrifice his sons.
My mother learned
a new language in her
late forties.
Leaving behind tailored dresses
and sparkling jewels.
Abandoned her status to work as a cook
at a beachfront hotel.

Her dainty feet swelled into boats,
never to recover.
Her mother tongue spoken to us,
while others did not understand her broken English.
Hope drifted in and out of
the windows of our home
and entered through the door one day.
But it was not long before a new hurdle
had to be confronted.
My mother and father
did not dwell in the past.
They lived every day
stung by the reality of
putting food on the table
and clothes on our backs.
Their love trickled in our sleep,
raised our dreams,
found a path,
to change,
to rise,
to recreate our life.

Confessions

Confessionals
leave me aching,
yearning
to lift the veil.
Unearth the secrets
from their burial ground,
of lullabies that are no longer mine.
A language forgotten,
where humanity and love merge.
Where light and grace dance as one.
Saddled by time,
the burden does not dissipate
nor die.
I told the sun about my demons,
the sun told the moon.
The moon lit my dark nights
and showed me the way
to a new dawn.

Tell Him

Son,
talk to your child
the way I spoke to you on moonless nights
about the stars and galaxies.
Tell him your tale:
how you loved cars and
how you simulated their sounds.
Tell him about colorful Lego bricks
you made into castles with soldiers,
about war and peace.
Tell your son
about the stories you devoured
of art and history,
how your home was filled with love,
and every breath was brimmed with gratitude.
Tell him about your ancestors
and their will to survive the
strife and hunger of the grey war.
Tell him about bees and pollination,
the salmon's migration,
grizzly bears,
and bald eagles.
Tell him of your struggles
and your human decency.
Talk to your son,
my child.
He will grow with sparkling pride.
He will know your love is undeniable,
he will feel
your love shining through his days and nights.

Woman

I discovered the crow's feet
nestled by my eyes.
I forgave them and accepted
them to be mine.
I love that they exhibit
a piece of my struggle.
Days I squinted in delight,
dark nights when weeping
left me drained and numb.
I questioned the veins in my hands,
pronounced and deep,
then I accepted them
for all the hard labor they had done.
Hands weathered by love given,
days from dawn to dusk,
babies they had washed,
foreheads caressed.
I watched my white strands
residing in my dark hair.
I accepted them for their resilience
and beauty.
I challenged my mind to battle the known,
and seek the wonder of the unknown.
I challenged my soul to rise up
and embrace the woman
I have become
and embrace the life I have been given.

Mid Life

My vessel empty, dark,
tangled up in sorrow.
My interior landscape, desolate,
the sound of the wind echoes through.
Days when I am the wreckage,
days when I am the storm.
Standing in mid-life,
the memory of the chaotic past floats
in and out of my thoughts,
like a colorful buoy
faded by the sun;
the color drained as the elements seized
without mercy.
The scars have faded but resurface
like a letter for additional postage.
Truth gnaws like a dog on a bone,
I choose to swim against the tides.
The erosion on my shore
only felt by me.
The mind battles the clutter,
while the illusions are mourned.
Tangled up in blue,
a light in the distance,
is the beacon,
to the answers,
to the possibility
of tomorrow.

What If I Forget?

The city I was born in,
my mother's maiden name,
the street I lived on.
Questions,
answers that do not warrant hesitation,
contemplation,
black and white,
nice and easy.
But what if I forget
one day,
my first pet's name,
my high school boyfriend,
and finding the love of my life.
What if it slips away,
like an oar in the river,
like water through my fingers,
like all the yesterdays
built by moments of you and me.
Holding hands,
speaking with our loud voices
at the spark of anger,
dancing in the kitchen,
our laughter echoes in our home.
Silent,
side by side at dawn,
our feet tangled
in a mess of love,
what if I forget?

Numbers-Holocaust

For Dad and Aunt Shelly

Numbers tattooed on my soul.
Lives snuffed out, erased,
roots of humanity pulled out like weeds,
so they would not grow,
or flourish,
so they would not survive.
Numbers tattooed,
like branded animals,
identities robbed,
discarded,
destroyed.
Voices silenced,
voices of philosophers,
poets,
bakers,
doctors,
mothers,
fathers,
children.
The old woman sits with me,
her eyes drift,
she remembers,
and she weeps.
she remembers walking into an empty house
for refuge,
a photograph
of a rabbi on the wall,
his blue eyes haunt her in her dreams.
She remembers hunger,
cold,
despair.

Her grandparents murdered,
her uncle vanished,
her aunt dismembered.
She is a part of me,
a piece of my legacy.
Her eyes are the same color
as my beloved father's eyes.
They held hands at the gates of hell
and survived.
I write down the stories,
seared with pain
of portraits of life ripped apart,
families lost,
unspeakable horrors.
I write stories,
I witness,
as tears fall down,
I hold her hand and,
we remember.

A Piece of Ourselves

The sun brazen,
honey colored,
gleamed through the door as he entered,
clutching bouquets of flowers.
Daisies, Lilies, Ginger
wild and beautiful.
I reached out for one,
the thorns of the rose pierced my skin,
reminding me that life was not always this way,
soft and loud with beauty.
The flower guy
was away in a mountain cabin,
writing his first novel.
I smile
understanding the struggle
of bleeding unto the page,
pouring our fears,
unveiling our truth,
weaving our words.
How softly we click on
the keys of our devices
writing feverishly.
Our minds holding boulders,
in the trenches of our thoughts,
fearful to leave on the page
more of ourselves than
we intended to.
I trim the flowers
on a slant,
place them in the
green and white crystal vase.
I cut my words
into shattered pieces of myself,

I place them on the page,
exposed.
I read them and
quickly I
erase and
start over.

Forgiveness

I forgave her for lying
and trying to steal my soul.
I forgave her for bringing storms into my days,
uncertainty in my steps,
and darkness in my hours.
I forgave her,
the sister I never had,
the confidante of secrets.
I brought her in from the rain, from a past,
embraced her brokenness unaware of her bite.
She loved me,
betrayed me,
said it was her illness.
She took my heart,
sliced it open
watched me bleed
as she stood motionless.
I saw her photograph
on the internet,
her eyes haunted,
a scar on her forehead,
a ghost of yesterday.
It was not her words
attempting to crawl back into the place she ravaged.
It was not her pleading voice on the answering machine.
I forgave her
to crawl out of the gutter
she placed us in.
I forgave her as I battled drowning in the outgoing tide.
I forgave her
to forgive myself.

Retrieved

The sound familiar
as it echoes through
the house.
The couch sighs,
the way it did when
she jumped off
to chase a squirrel
in the yard,
or follow me
when I walked away.
The memory recovered,
the way she retrieved sticks on autumn days.
Her nose wet,
red collar,
unbridled joy,
shaking the raindrops
as she swayed.
She faintly smelled like trees,
she wagged her tail,
while words of poetry
danced on the page.
Outside the window,
leaves are scattered,
the homeless cat can
no longer tell her tales,
of the birds she hunts,
and duck eggs left unattended
for moments at a time.
She daydreamed,
we daydreamed,
side by side.

One Hundred Years Armenian Genocide

For Grandpa Antranik
A poem dedicated to my husband and his grandfather.

Coal black sky,
awakens repressed memories.
Whispers of angels silenced.
You are not forgotten,
the moon watched
while humanity looked away,
one hundred years of denial.
Grandpa,
I stood beside you as a boy,
and as a man, I carry you in my heart.
Your kind but dark eyes,
pieced my consciousness with stories of your plight,
living in a cave,
marching in the desert,
eating weeds and plants.
You were a baby boy orphaned,
grief held your hand.
You were too young to remember your mother's love
your mother's embrace.
The emptiness,
and the sadness lingered.
The oppressors sought to destroy,
they sought deportation, humiliation,
death.
The oppressors wished
to erase you
and our bloodline.
One hundred years of denial,
echo like whispers,
reverberate from the earth
of those that perished.

You survived
to flourish
you survived
to tell your story
the darkness always in the shadows
of each day.
Grandpa,
I remember.
Grandpa,
your words are not forgotten,
I retell my children of those dark days,
of their legacy,
of survival rich with
honor of your life.
Grandpa,
I stood beside you as a child,
as a man I carry you in my heart.

Remember and Change

Dad,
I don't want to write about spring,
flowers blooming,
touching my skin,
making my spirits rejoice.
Dad,
I don't wish to write about egrets flying into my yard,
celebrating glorious blue skies.
Dad,
I want to write about hunger and pain,
about a dark time,
when the sun did not shine for you and for others.
A time when your belly was empty,
and your eyes witnessed
horrors that remained with you
till the day you died.
I don't want to be gentle or soft,
I want to awaken souls.
I want the world to remember,
humanity at its worst.
I want them to know
that you did not
let it define you.
You were a survivor,
a champion,
that fought for other people's rights.
Your heart open,
and your mind filled with dreams.
You wrote beautiful words,
soaring above the pain and horror.
Dad,
I want them to remember,
the people that perished,

the people that did not
get to have
a new life.
I want the world to remember.

Silence

Hesitations,
confrontations,
conversations.
Crumbs leftover from yesterday, fear induced.
I am sliced paper thin
by questions and self-doubt.
Hesitations,
conversations,
truth,
words dancing on the page.
Complications,
hesitations,
thoughts percolating,
truth illuminating the way.
Silence,
suffocating,
drowning,
casting shadows and
darkness.
If I recall our story
with truth and beauty,
unveil it with clarity and charity,
will you let me
raise my chest into the air.
Will you let the steam and fire rise,
and let me spin my words that
saturate life.
Will you let me,
breathe secrets into the universe
or will you silence me?

Enchantment

For Aiden

Your sweetness
awakens peace within me,
an immense joy
that roars like incoming
waves breaking on the shore.
The tides rise and fall
with time,
as I look into your eyes
and our souls meet again.
My words palpable
pour on to the page
unassuming
brimming with enchantment
and truth.
You nestled in my heart,
my love for you,
pure,
immeasurable.
I wait for the universe to lift you,
embrace you
and write the chapters of your life
with peace,
felicity,
and enlightenment.

Precious One

For Aiden

May the sound of the sea
give you tranquility.
May the sight of the blue topaz sky
spark your desire to fly.
May you bloom like a flower
on the side of the mountain resilient and graceful.
May your steps be light
and your touch gentle.
May you be strong like
the roots of the oak tree.
May you find the sacred in the ordinary,
in the light breeze on your face,
in the crimson sunrise,
in the salty taste of the ocean spray.
May you delight in powerful words.
may you be charmed by sweet poetry.
May you play in the moonlight,
sketch on the large canvas of life,
bathe underneath the stars.
May you dream big.
Love fiercely.
Laugh,
Laugh,
and laugh some more.

Aiden Karl Ethan

Hello world
he seemed to say
with one eye open
as he gazed at life.
Seven pounds
fifteen ounces
infant warrior.
Hello snow,
blizzard raging.
Hello mother,
father,
grandmas,
hello nurses,
doctors.
Hello world,
wrinkly fingers and toes,
dimples,
footprints engraved on our souls.
Hello world,
sucking noises,
sighs,
sweet cries,
the sounds of the Wheels on the bus,
Abc's,
paw prints on the sidewalk.
Hello world,
breath,
love,
peace,
I am Aiden,
and
I am ready to step into this world,
and
embrace it all.

Little One

For Aiden

What do you see in your dreams little one?
sheep that you count
white and dreamy
like the billowy clouds above.
What do you see in your dreams
when you sigh in your sleep,
green endless fields,
yellow and black Labrador retrievers?
Do you smile because you see
your mother and father gazing
at you with adoration
sparkle in their eyes.
Do you dream about
your maternal and paternal grandmothers
rocking you to sleep gently and lovingly.
What do you see in your dreams
little one?
The sun shining through
the gray morning
as the snow melts off
the bare trees
outside your window.
Milk and sweetness
life and love.
Do you see the future smiling on you,
what do you see my love?

Breaking the Chain

For Carl and Garo

Dad,
I stand before you a man, inward a young boy,
a spectator of our life.
The man has no expectations, the boy remembers.
You left me on the shore,
like husks and shells
that you stepped on.
The boy remembers shining
to your blind eyes.
Your acceptance
not felt, nor voiced.
Your arms never stretched
to raise me,
to lift me.
My stories were chatter,
you did not want to hear.
Sound bytes buried
as you became increasingly irritated by the tone
of my voice.
You were deaf,
your mind self absorbed.
Whores and drugs seduced you,
friends and the bottle captured your attention.
I was an afterthought,
oblivious to my needs
you lacked empathy.
I searched for light in your eyes,
I waited for a kind word,
but encouragement and respect
were not in your vocabulary.
Dad,
I stand before you

as a man,
as a father.
I am not you,
your errors and indifference shaped me,
your road-map not my own.
The sounds of my children are the dearest
to me,
their pain is mine to carry.
No task too great, no sacrifice enough.
I encourage,
I nurture,
I lift,
I broke the chain.

I Am an Immigrant—I Am an American

Bury me in a pine box
breathless yet breathing.
I won't leave,
I won't go.
I rested my weary head
on her shoulders.
Her courage,
became my own.
I swam in her oceans,
I climb her hills and mountains.
I swore my loyalty,
my allegiance.
Her flag engraved across
my heart,
the stars and stripes my own.
I brimmed with emotion
and devotion.
Her outstretched arms
embraced me,
took me in.
She whispered words of inclusion,
she roared words of freedom
and love.
I am not a stranger,
this is my home.
I am an American,
I won't leave,
I won't go.

Sixteen

For Daniel

Sixteen is the handsome boy
that feels like an ugly duckling.
Sixteen is wise remarks
that make me laugh
even though I restrain myself.
Sixteen is dark humor
mixed with silly undertones.
It's tousled curls in his hair
when it was always lank.
Sixteen is a world
I want to step into
as I sink into a marsh.
I try to remember
my sixteen,
my youth,
my insecurities,
and struggle
to mirror his uncharted sea.
Sixteen is loving
in small gestures,
it's late nights,
boundless energy,
it's heavy and light.
Sixteen
is sinking into a computer screen
for endless hours,
talking to friends
while saying nothing
of importance.
Sixteen
resides in a room
that resembles a dungeon.

The only beacon are keepsakes buried in the closet
and chest
of drawers.
He is witty like Stephen Colbert
and funny like Jon Stewart
not that I would compare him to either.
He is unique,
this sixteen unparalleled
to any other.
This is his path to walk on,
and mine to follow from a distance with unconditional love.

Let Sadness In

Let sadness
transform you,
trickle down from
your head to your toes.
Let it widen your chest and raise your heart.
Let sadness dance
in your veins,
a slow dance,
a deliberate dance.
Open the window,
let it in, let it sit for a while.
Let it soak in your bones,
let it ravage you.
It will travel through
the chambers of your heart,
and your soul.
It will leave you feeble at the knees like a gentle lover.
It will dissolve like fog at daybreak over the harbor.
You will grow
from the heartache,
you will weather the storm.
You will survive,
you will find joy.

Her Hands

I don't recognize these hands
blemished and wrinkled.
These hands
were attached to my body
for twenty years
while I slept.
I awake to find them asking,
why I am reluctant to claim them.
They ask
why I pretend to be
a patient with temporary amnesia.
I don't recognize these hands,
they washed dishes,
changed soiled diapers, turned pages,
and touched fevered foreheads.
Mom had beautiful hands,
even when she passed away
at eighty years old.
She rubbed them
with cream from Switzerland
after she finished
chores,
baked and cooked,
hung up her day,
like a coat on a hanger.
Mom caressed her hands,
as faint luxurious scent
floated in the air.
Mom had beautiful hands,
not I.

Grandson

Grandson,
I dream of holding your
sweet slumber in my arms.
Your hair wild,
your eyes luminous.
My finger laced
in yours.
My thoughts
swept away,
unravel with hope
and wonder.
You are a mystery,
I have yet to discover.
My heart beats
with anticipation.
Grandson,
I await
to greet you,
to look into your angelic eyes,
to touch your tender skin.
We have not met
but I love you
your footprints are engraved
on my heart.
Your breath,
your life,
a celebration
of adoration.
We have not met yet
but I love you.

Redemption

Stripped of my vanity,
I wear you like a crown,
strands of white
downy floating on the sides of my face.
Gentle like the wind, gentle like my soul,
I am comfortable
in my skin,
unveiling scars of shame,
and hushed confessions.
The crow's feet are seen,
I do not wish to hide them,
or erase them.
The mirror does not lie,
nor do I.
My narrative
is mine to tell.
We all have one,
or two.
I walked alone,
I did not fear the unknown.
Curiosity and wonder
were my companions.
I wear my failures
on my skin,
on the map of my soul,
in my dark eyes
and my enlightened being.

Mom

There was a comfort
knowing that I could hear
your voice,
melt into your arms,
watch the shadows cast
on your face,
and know how to bring
light into your eyes.
There was comfort in loving,
in living,
in a shared meal,
an anecdote,
in silent moments.
There was comfort
I no longer find,
the one I felt in your womb
or your gentle hand
on my burning forehead
when I was sick.
I have no church or synagogue to find refuge in.
I seek the museums
of the world
where we once walked together,
I walk alone.
In their splendor
I feel you like a gentle wind
beside me,
urging me to see the magnificence.
The art fills my soul
with curiosity and wonder.
I find you there,
loving me,
giving me the will
to find the essence
in the beauty of this life.

Unvarnished

The mirror shards,
sharp as the strands of grey hair,
unvarnished
like the redwood trees.
You would not recognize
the resilient starfish
left on the shore
to die.
You were a stray dog
that followed me home.
I let you into
my consciousness.
You wagged your tail,
you licked my face
with adoration
before you barked.
When you bit me,
I put you down.
I was sober,
you were not.
I was not a muñequita
to chew and spit out.
Blindfolded I was lured
by the darkness,
misery I mired in.
You set fire and scorched
our landscape.
I rose from the ashes,
while you
became a ghost of the past.

The Color of My Blood

For the victims and survivors of Pulse nightclub
in Orlando and their families

The shape of my eyes,
the sound of my voice,
the shade of my skin,
my sexuality.
The color of my blood
the same
as yours.
If you saw the light in my eyes,
if you saw my mother's tears,
if you felt her fears,
grief engraved on her skin.
Would you have yanked me like a weed from the garden of life,
Would you have shattered me in pieces
leaving me
to bleed out in the dark.
Ideologies differ,
dreams unalike,
my diversity
makes me
unique,
beautiful,
majestic,
a beacon in the fiber
of humanity.
The shape of my eyes,
the sound of my voice,
the shade of my skin,
my sexuality.
The color of my blood the same as yours.

Boundaries

For Josh

I savor the snapshots of our life,
a little boy's laughter,
angelic and sweet.
We were two peas in a pod,
smiling as we welcomed the night,
books by the bedside,
your little finger curled
in the tangle of my hair,
as you pleaded for one more story.
I was your cheerleader,
in games lost,
in dreams nurtured and sustained.
I wanted to see the world
through your eyes,
not mine.
You taught me lessons
in ordinary moments,
that gracefully were extraordinary.
You taught me that there is
no other option but
the naked truth.
I should have known
that your world
would become larger
and that mine would be smaller,
that life would be complicated,
a new path
mapped with boundaries.
The storms that I endured,
would be kernels of wisdom,
to let go,
to step back,
to watch you stand on your own.

Your Beating Heart

The black bird carried a twig to the nest,
the shimmering light reflected over the lake.
Spring entered our home and our subconscious,
yet I have not stopped
to welcome the sounds of the earth awakening,
dreamily stretching.
I've been nourishing
and nurturing
those that I love.
I have been sadder
than they can understand
and stronger than I can comprehend.
I have been living in the past
more than in the moment,
feeling the helplessness
of the way time floats through
my hands and my days.
Moments that we can't get more of,
days once wasted,
lost and gone.
I've been stretching my limbs,
my mind diluted.
The wind murmurs in my ear,
"You are strong,"
I answer,
"Have you not seen my tears,
heard my defeat,
felt the weakness from my wounds."
The wind caresses me,
I run through the torrents of rain,
listening to the uplifting guidance,
longing to hear
the sound of your beating heart.

Unwanted

I don't remember if the Palm fronds swayed
outside the window.
I don't remember
what day it was.
Her words spilled like
salt grains,
without reservation
or anticipation nor regret.
Her words froze
in mid-air
and as they melted
into my consciousness
I looked into her eyes
to recognize a glimmer of regret.
It was simply
laid out
for me to examine and explore.
She was not going to keep me
she was not
going to give me life.
I was a pawn in life's chess game,
sour slices of memory seared
my being and
floated to the surface.
I remember the hollow feeling,
the feverish way
my skin tingled
as it broke into a rash.
She loved me,
but she did not want me.
As I digested
her words
I wondered
if she could ever understand

how she altered my world.
If I had not lived
what would her
snow globes look like,
dark with slush
or shimmering with light.
She would not have known
a daughter's
love
nor the gentle words in which she
cradled life.
I held her hand when she took
her last breath,
she never understood
why her words pierced my soul.
She never understood how she altered my world.

Free

Carolina chickadee flew into the park
one brilliant morning.
The trees rejoiced,
their leaves swaying
to the autumn breeze.
I tasted change looming,
as my eyes softly
welcomed them
with a smile.
I harbor memories
of long ago,
on a distant shore
of the caged small birds
chirping,
feasting passionately
from a sugar bowl
oblivious to their circumstance.
The bartender said
they were love birds
and they mate for life.
He poured rum into a tall glass
while sand brushed my toes.
I laughed,
I remember my innocence.
Youth and it's delicious
and painful blunders,
a lifetime ago.
I sigh,
my thirst for life and love
awakened my resolve.
My rebellion,
my transformation,
from a girl into a woman,
A woman that would become a mother,

that loved fiercely.
A woman that believed in dreams
and starting over.
A woman that wanted to touch
the sky
like a free bird.

A Queen
for Angel

We bought brown suede boots,
durable and rugged.
We bought the boots
to wear them to the field,
when we ran with our dog.
She was a puppy then
running with joyful abandon,
chasing shadows,
and her tail.
I lost myself in her gaze,
deep and steady.
She curled up next to me,
leaving no space for anyone else.
She was graceful, as if
she knew that she was
a queen in another life,
and I was her servant.
He misses her,
and he misses the young
girl that I used to be.

Gone

When I am gone,
I want to dwell in your dreams,
like a fluttering butterfly landing
on your skin.
I want to kiss your eyelids when you sleep,
and embrace you with my wings.
When I am gone,
I will dance with you
through the continents,
we will hopscotch through the stars,
as we climb into
each other's arms.
When I am gone,
I will leave my scent on your pillow,
while the violins play,
and while you drink poems for breakfast
in a tall cup,
knowing you were loved.

Fear

Fear whispered in my ears,
like a mosquito feasting on my skin.
It whispered doubts,
it challenged me into a battle
on the field of life.
I left fear on the sidelines of youth,
and it found me in mid-life.
It entered like a burglar
on a dark night,
awakened me in my sleep,
and shined a bright light
in my eyes.
It stood over me
as my heart raced.
Fear climbed the fence
of my garden
and planted seeds
while my back was turned,
like a needle piercing my subconscious.
Fear touched my wounds,
injured my being.
It whispered,
it whispered,
then it roared.

Heart

For Carl

You know my heart,
the hallways and corridors.
You walked through,
brushing
the walls,
touching my lust and melancholy,
my addiction and joy.
You know my heart,
how it beats to your embrace,
how it dances around your moon.
You have heard the thunder
of my heart,
the rivers of my veins pulsating
as you swam through them,
floating lost in the shadows,
familiar with the hidden fears.
You know my heart,
it beats to your touch,
it climbs to meet you,
it holds you close.

Grace in the Moments

I savor small bites of happiness,
leaving some for other days.
Days unfolding with grace,
moments undefined and simple,
the kind that flow through my hands
like running water.
Those are the moments
I remember at 4 A.M
when I can't sleep,
and you embrace me
in your half sleep,
our bodies forming a crescent moon.
The days sometimes escape me,
hours playing hide and seek
but the moments
leave me dazzled and spent.
Glorious they stand on their own
two feet.

Forgiveness and the Long Way Home

I had a red shiny tricycle, but never a bicycle.
I dreamt of riding free,
in a yellow lemon dress,
flying down the hill
with the wind caressing my hair.
Dad feared I would fall
and I would hurt myself.
So I didn't fly until years later, when I ran away,
no longer accepting to be sheltered from the storms of life.
I left with a plane ticket,
the clothes on my back,
and a dream in my heart.
My purse was stuffed with family photographs
that I treasured,
memories of what I was leaving behind.
No money
or plans,
the man sitting next to me on the plane spoke
about pre-Colombian art,
puzzled, he watched the stars in my eyes.
My life was waiting,
forbidden love,
youth, brilliant and reckless.
Seduced by a freedom fighter,
not knowing he worshiped methadone,
hidden away in the refrigerator.
When John Lennon was shot
I still believed in the change that never came.
I battled his demons
and lost.
Broken dreams and promises.
I woke up one day and walked
away with my soul battered
but not defeated.

I walked away
and opened new doors
and dreamt new dreams
fire in my soul
the wind on my back.

Refuge

I bow to the trees,
the chirping birds are my choir.
I find refuge in silent fields,
immunity unspoken,
wounds barely healed,
redemption afforded.
I have forgiven you,
but not myself.
"Not possible," you exclaim,
the ache is throbbing,
the mind is searching,
answers are far and few.
Don't ask me if I want to live,
ask me if I choose to die.

Waiting to Grow Up

The sidewalk had traces of pink and yellow chalk,
sounds echoed of hopscotch played yesterday.
My footsteps heavy,
sadness in my heart
locked away.
I thought about the war,
sirens in the night,
silent in the dark bomb shelter,
a ladybug crawling on my arm.
There was a boy in school,
with big brown eyes,
his locks curled gently.
He never saw me,
he was three years older.
I wonder if he is an old man now,
or if he died in battle.
I knew love would come one day,
exquisite,
heartbreaking,
glorious love.
We left home
my brothers all grown,
they attempted to shield me
from scraped knees,
broken bones,
and reality.
They could not see
how sad my smile was,
and how deep my thoughts were.
We crossed the ocean and planted our lives
like roots of a tree into a new society.
I was mesmerized at the pace,
instant macaroni and cheese in
a blue and yellow box,

television loud with color and life.
There were egg-shaped tape players,
and boats bobbing in the bay,
and large spaces in between.
The sound of the waves in the ocean
lulled me to sleep.
I was dreaming,
all along,
waiting to grow up.

Beloved

Beloved,
if I forget you,
let death carry me
on her shoulders.
If I forget you, let
the walls of my heart
be desolate,
let the sounds of my soul be
 silent.
If I forget you
there would be no reason to live,
you are the heartbeat,
you are the flame,
you are the fire.

Daniel

Books on the shelves,
live in your being,
dancing in your thoughts.
You have devoured the pages,
lost in their magic.
Your imagination
filled with colors,
a kaleidoscope of life,
your wisdom beyond your years.
My eyes delight in
your walk,
you are
tall and limber,
no longer a boy
but a young man.
Your voice nourishes
my soul,
your laughter is the soundtrack
of my days.
I celebrate today,
your birthday.
I celebrate every giggle,
and sound every day
with love
and gratitude
and wonder.

The Sigh of the Roots

My beloved,
plant me an orange tree
it's nectar sweet on my lips.
Follow me to the orange grove barefoot and free.
In the orange grove
grandma's spirit lives,
in the sigh of the trees,
in the wondrous soil.
That is where she held
people's hands,
and people's lives,
and inspired them to love her
the way she was meant to be loved.
My beloved,
Husband,
tender heart,
know that these are my roots
that I have walked this far,
and I have learned lessons of life
in the charred limbs of a tree,
in the puzzle patches of the bark,
in the eyes of the Cooper's Hawk greeting me with love.
Plant me an orange tree
and forever I will
be grateful.

What Remains

What remains is
the vast blue sky,
words in tattered notebooks,
love softly engraved on the skin,
where it was born,
cultivated,
and freed.
What remains of my life is
the love I gave,
with outstretched arms,
with my heart blooming,
to make yours rise.
What remains is laughter
carried by the wind,
feathers floating in the park.
What remains are the
moon and the stars,
as the days go forward,
and life goes on.

Grace

I drink from the silver Amethyst chalice
seeking communion.
The roof shelters me while I wonder if
the cobwebs on my soul are seen from the heavens.
I walk along the shadows,
silence is a death sentence.
Life lingers on my lips
awakened by the sounds
and colors of poetry,
shaking my senses,
leading me home.
Grace floats unannounced,
it walks lacing her
arm into mine.
Grace never tarnished,
stands alone
on wings of hope,
failure is a lesson.

Surrender

Wash my feet
sweet ocean,
to you, I surrender.
Your lips soothing
like a lullaby
whispered to an infant.
Angels sing,
and poets dream.
I am awakened
by this moment,
ordinary
yet extraordinary.
My feet anchored in the sand,
seashells leave a mysterious trail.
Life is here,
connected to all that came before us,
and all that remains.
I inhale,
I exhale,
I surrender.

Farewell

For Captain Farrell and Garo Zarfjian

The ocean holds our dreams,
waves have washed over us
while we trolled the great ocean,
as it unfolded and lay in front
of us in its glory.
These waves tender
and fierce
told our stories to the sun,
the moon,
and the vast sky.
We were one with the currents and the tides.
We watched birds working,
our guides to clues.
Our reels sang
as we fished,
your laughter
genuine and loud,
while joy flowed in our veins.
Images of yesterday stir my soul,
tears falling
for a friend that was a brother
to me.
While the fishing rods sway
to the rhythm
of the universe
our friendship
lasted to the sunset of our life.

Ralph

For my dear friend Ralph Epstein

The owl watches me from his burrow,
"good morning,"
I whisper
as not to arouse suspicion of my sanity
to others.
His eyebrows
prominent white,
his eyes shine.
He is shaded by
a great old tree
with giant roots,
and a giant heart,
the kind old trees possess .
The red flowers shed
on the ground,
are like a carpet as I walk by.
The owl watches me,
and others that
go past him,
without a second glance.
I think about an old friend,
his hair was grey,
and his enthusiasm unmatched
by any young folks.
He was awarded
a purple heart, and
the Bronze Star
with three oak leaf clusters for valor,
for bravery he exhibited
during world war II.
He told jokes,

and he was delighted when I listened,
and I smiled.
He offered help
when he saw me drowning,
and he wept with me when his mother died
in her late nineties.
He lived and died
on his own terms,
courageous and full of spirit.
When I heard the news
I wept,
a wound left inside me.
I think of him often,
he was one of those souls
that are rare,
and kind
gentle and giant.
His soul saw mine,
like the great tree in this park with a huge heart,
like this owl that
watches me
as if he can see
my soul.
Connections,
chance encounters,
spirits entwined as one,
for a moment
for a day,
forever.

Sanity

I walk through the trees
observing light and shadow.
I feel the inspiration stir,
awaken,
I take a breath watching
a butterfly follow me.
I breathe words these days,
but they are silenced
by my questioning heart
asking does it matter?
Do I matter?
The saturated fear
that it does not
leave me empty like
a husk I see on the ground.
I question my sanity,
my worth,
I disrobe of the accolades
and strip bare.
It's all been said
and done,
light and shadow dual,
I struggle,
my soul had been cracked
open before.
I claw out of the darkness
to see the sun.
I kneel by the ocean
and question the smallness of it all
in this vast world.
I am small,
I am humbled,
I am a whisper.

Nothing

I am the whisper on your lips.
I am the silence accepting communion.
I am a weed in the rose garden.
I am a husk in the green field.
I am driftwood washed to shore.
I am a grain of sand.
I am a whitecap
in the breaking waves of the ocean.
I am the morning dew on the maple leaf.
I am nothing,
without you.

The Hunger

The secrets of the sea,
contained in a shell,
the wind whispers ours.
The hunger alive,
words in the grains of the earth.
I seek truth,
watching the birds diving,
fishing for iridescent fish,
they know the secrets of the world.
You cast with anticipation,
bright eyes,
the eternal boy that knows
his way to the lighthouse
in the stormy sea.
The waves fierce and tender,
unknown mysteries,
that will
never reveal themselves.
Yet,
I am the seeker,
the wanderer,
the poet,
the mother,
wondering,
questioning,
always hungry for more.

The Tree of Blood

Sadness evokes memories,
morning dew on leaves forsaken.
Light penetrating,
piercing the morning
with a new promise.
A moment held through time,
threads of our tapestry
that were unraveled,
and forgotten.
Where have we gone wrong,
lost our keen,
and our desire to know our blood.
Am I the only one to celebrate
the roots of our tree.
The roots that had spread
to different lands,
planting seeds,
and building new worlds,
only to forget the ones
that spilled their blood,
and their desire for us to survive,
and escape hate and oppression.
The threads frayed,
the threads in desperate
need of repair.
I am the one consumed
with the tales,
the history,
the need to remember.
My heart
like bruised grapes,

soft and tender,
beating in anticipation.
I am the weed left behind,
resilient,
seeking the light.

Through the Fog

The wind carried the sound
of my weeping,
scattered dandelions floating away.
My grief broke me open,
brought me to my knees.
My thoughts,
waves of despair
and sorrow.
I was told that I should numb my pain
with pills,
with wine,
with life.
I refused
I soaked it in,
I swam in it,
I drowned.
The grief
let my heart bleed,
the blade deep and sharp.
My thoughts consumed me,
I surrendered
to my anguish.
Every morning the sun rose,
and I learned to walk through
the sorrow unhinged,
undone.
I slept on a bed of thorns,
the darkness draping me.
I walked the path,
on shattered glass.
I fell into grief and honored it.
Moments,
hours,
days,

months went by.
One day the sun rose,
my burden felt lighter.
I chose to rise from the ashes,
and find glory in the morning light,
in the love in my life,
in remembering that you
would want me to live,
and breathe again.
I chose to live
among the glory that
is in a new day,
the only day that's promised.

Here

The city vibrant,
loud and familiar.
The moon watches over us,
knowingly lighting our way.
A homeless man,
laying on the ground holding a cup,
while he recites poetry about a yellow canoe.
Schizophrenic, or perhaps he is saner than all of us.
His voice loud and clear,
yet gentle.
I am filled with emotion,
tears well up
of old wounds
I have forgotten.
At the museum
we explore the beauty,
a little boy
weeps,
while he hangs on to his mother's arm,
as if he was drowning
and she is his life preserver.
My thoughts drift
to sleepless nights,
and restless days.
I look away and
fight the tears
because I love you more
than you can ever understand.
Our time here brief,
this is where I want to be
in this beautiful city that you call home.
You work from ten to seven,
all night,
caring for humanity,

while the moon crawls to greet me
through the window.
I sleep and dream
of my wide-eyed boy
tending to those never cared for,
uprooted and lost.
The past is calling
but I choose today.
I choose this moment
bittersweet yet glorious.

The Apple Tree

Dad wrote poems for mom,
and he read them aloud to her.
I listened,
while they thought that
I was sleeping.
His voice filled with passion
and love.
Dad wrote me stories,
about a horse with a broken leg.
It was published
in the newspaper.
Life was art to him,
and art was life.
I watched him mesmerized,
he was bigger than life,
crowds were captivated by
his presence.
Mom said that the apple does not fall far from the tree,
and that I was like him.
I wanted to write poetry like him,
and love like him.
His flame burning.
His thirst of life, never quenched,
his hunger
never satiated.
He never followed anyone,
he always followed his instinct.
His seeds of wisdom
ingrained in my being.
His life was filled with sadness
and despair during the war.
The obstacles never defined him,
he rose and overcame
to build a life that was well lived.

Mom said that I was strong as steel,
when I went through my journey.
I told her that the strength was born out of necessity.
My bloodlines rich with struggle
and endurance.
I think of them,
and honor the place that
I come from,
and the apple tree I fell out of.

An Olive Branch

The canopy of trees layered,
the leaves sway to an
invisible symphony dancing,
wearing crowns
like the layers of my heart.
In my green peridot field,
in the orange grove,
I planted seeds of hope,
seeds for peace.
I found the walls and distance between us,
all the reasons why we are the same,
instead of different.
I planted seeds with my bare soul,
the words that sprouted were hopeful
like an olive branch offering.
You half smiled and half mocked,
my hopeful dream.
Verse sprinkled with
wonder and pain.
Layers of life risen from the trenches,
soaring to enlightenment.
The leaves are dancing
in the breeze,
like words of truth that I stuffed
into my soul.
Bleeding unto the page,
soaking my bones,
like the water soaking
the seeds I left behind,
to saturate and grow.
Words that liberate,
words that set us free.

Awaken

The hunger weeps in the night,
what will you do to wake up your soul,
what you will do to awaken mine?
Desire filled nights,
our hearts racing,
as we wait for dawn's light.
I washed my soul in the ocean
while tears fell tenderly.
Your fingers ran down my spine,
and left a print on my skin.
Your arms a homecoming,
sun-kissed days
that ached in sweet surrender.
You are the dew on the morning grass,
you are the sound of the rustling leaves,
you are the wine in my empty glass.
What will you do to wake up your soul,
What will you do to awaken mine.

Fearless

"Our bodies
carry our biographies,"
she says,
her voice gentle and soothing
as she instructs us into
a yoga pose.
The walls are green,
a mix of
jade and avocado.
Our bodies remember where we have been
and who we are.
They hold the scars and shame.
I breathe
and remember the collisions
of my soul.
My body remembers
that I've been beaten,
even though my scars have faded.
It remembers despair
and hunger in my darkest moments.
I was a fearless young girl
that followed her heart.
I have traveled the road
of humiliation and determination,
highs and lows.
My body remembers
the joy of the birth of my children,
holding them for the first time
as my soul lifted.
My heart remembers
the sorrow of my parents dying,
the conflicts of religion
and spirituality.
The hopscotch between

two continents
that were both home to me.
The anxiety and loneliness
until I built a new world.
My soul rises,
it's always known where I belong
and how I feel.
I always knew,
I never needed to search
for my identity.
I have followed
my heart.
My words have guided me,
lifted me,
gave me a voice.
I wish to leave the words behind,
not half-truths
but honest confessions.
I want to wear my shame
as well as I wear my triumphs.
My love will linger in my
boys' hearts and
on my lover's lips.
My love is what defines me.

Your Books

I found your seeds of wisdom,
in my subconscious where you buried them
long ago.
Along with seeds
of love, that you gave me
every time our eyes met.
I found your books,
overflowing boxes,
in rooms
smelling like the old and the new
in a wonderful mixture
of life.
Sober from the loss,
I gave your books away,
as if they were casual friends
we did not want to dine with.
I gave them away
and I felt empty.
You had extracted beauty
from their pages,
while you were famished for knowledge.
They gave you the breath
of life,
and silenced your desires.
Words that you carried,
multifaceted gems of light,
when you spoke,
I could see their brilliance.
I sat in the dark room,
wishing I could wallpaper the walls
with the contents of art,
philosophy,
and poetry,

sentences you strung with passion.
I sat hoping that I would catch a whisper,
of your voice calling.
When I closed my eyes,
silence persisted.
I held your shirt
breathing in your faint scent.
I sat and I waited,
feeling you closer,
all along,
the moon comforting me.

Never Again

I stand at the edge of the world,
where the clouds
and shadows meet.
The darkness draws me in,
an echo resonating in my being.
The war was long,
and heartless.
Innocence lost,
lives perished,
rays of light dimmed.
Names will be called
in Berlin, Jerusalem,
Boston,
Washington D.C.
as we whisper under our breath,
the words,
never again.
The sound of the names called
will make us shudder,
leave us empty,
and somber.
Their stories are mine, their loss is ours.
My great grandparents were murdered
in cold blood,
their blood is still pulsating in my veins.
The roots of my tree have been cut down,
forever changed.
I lost my religion,
but I never lost hope.
I will not forget,
I will not walk away,
I will not be silenced.
I will wear the yellow
star on my heart for them.

We were not connected only
by religion
but by humanity.
I will remember,
they are engraved
on the walls of my heart.
Never again
I whisper.

Daniel and the Blushing Moon

The lizard tells me tales about the dragonfly,
while it chases shadows under the palm trees.
The worms are crawling in the mud,
whispering about last night.
We gazed at the sky and we watched
the lunar eclipse mesmerized.
Holding the lens,
capturing the
blood moon blushing.
The color vibrant,
and our hearts open.
There is a silent truth
in moments like these.
I watch you immersed
in wonder,
and the stillness and magic
of it all,
and it saturates my being
with gratitude
and celebration.

Treasures

The box of jewels
is dressed in green velvet inside.
The box is home to the leaves,
and shells that you gave me.
They chatter all day,
when the house is silent,
I listen.
The leaves remember the taste of rain.
They whisper of spring and children in the park.
They whisper of vines crawling,
bathing in the sunlight.
The shells tell tales
about mermaids with wavy hair,
floating on seaweed and frolicking in the waves.
We walked along the sand,
the pail was full,
those summer days we shared on the island.
Your hair smelled
like the salty sea.
I took a deep breath
taking it in,
like oxygen
to carry me through.
I chased the days
as they slipped away,
like water rolling through my hands.
The leaves and shells chatter,
and I remember
magical yesterdays.

The Dragon
Daniel and The Perez Museum

The light shimmers
on the water.
The museum stands
like a jewel on the waterfront.
We watch the egrets
spread their wings,
slowly, powerfully,
and we dream of freedom.
Our thoughts floating away with them.
You are born on the year of the dragon,
myth and legend.
Symbol of power and good fortune.
Your eyes shine the way the stars
illuminate the night,
and your strength is in your words,
and in your hunger.
One day you will
make this a better place,
with your vision
and your wisdom.
You will be carried
by your wings stretching to
embrace the wondrous universe.

Cast Net Memories

I threw a cast net
into the universe,
and captured shards,
filled with memories,
that made me who I am today.
You threw a cast net into the ocean,
and caught fish flailing,
dancing for your mercy,
and their freedom.
I told you secrets,
I watched you hold your breath, and
I waited for you to exhale.
When you did,
I danced in your light,
standing away from the shadows,
letting you in the door,
of the narratives
and darkness that I carried within.
I didn't fear your judgment,
I only feared that your love would wilt
and die.

Spring of Humanity

The seeds of spring
take me into the journey within.
The colors are the backdrop
to the thoughts taking flight.
I watch the ripples in the pond of humanity.
We hunger to tell our tale,
to share our vision,
to dream,
to nourish our souls.
To hope,
that life can be different.
We share ourselves
bits and pieces, all along
hiding our true story,
while we drink wine
and taste morsels of life,
our road blurred
by our broken compass.
The hunger lives,
the fragments like the
new leaves sprouting.
The scent of spring is in the air,
underneath the surface, the desire is rising,
seeking to convey,
seeking to connect.
Our well waiting to bubble.
I watch with intention,
I inhale the light,
my landscape
full of this moment,
and the stories of humanity.

Small
Reuven Rubin

We traveled to his home,
on the narrow coastal plain
along the Mediterranean sea.
It was nestled in Caesarea,
where the sunset
took my breath away.
The blue sky filled with pink,
and an inviting orange.
I was seven or eight,
but I was an old soul.
I felt like I carried the
world on my shoulders.
The party inside
was all that I had imagined,
except I remained outside,
with my brother and the chauffeur.
Mom said that I was too young,
which made me feel small.
I wanted to walk among his art
and breathe it in.
Wander into a painting,
and feel the sand under my feet.
I wanted to feel his art,
seeping from his walls giving life
to his famous Galilean hills.
His view harmonious,
and his reality filled
with grace,
in which foes could be friends.
I wanted to look into the fire
in his eyes,
knowing it came from deep inside his soul.

His passion
that brought life
to blank canvases filled with color.
He was inspired by frescoes,
his vision
not just seen but felt.
I wanted to listen
to the conversation,
about life in Paris,
and his first exhibition in New York.
Bridges he built from the past
to a future he dreamed of.
I wanted to know
about being uprooted,
and blooming in a new land
and society.
I wanted to hear the sounds,
and pretend
not to listen to whispers
when the conversation became edgy.
His art and life were one,
and I understood that.
Mom said that I was too young,
which made me feel small.

You Are

For Mom and Dad

You are the feather that finds me,
and rests on my shoulder.
You are the breeze
that caresses my skin.
You are the shimmer I see over clear waters.
You are the fearless butterfly
that lands on my face.
You are the sound that I hear from the music box,
while no one touched it.
You are the seagull poised
on the fence,
anchored in the moment.
You are the song
the sparrow sings.
You are the joy and sorrow
I feel within.
You are in my smile,
in the sound of my laughter,
in the core of my being.

Andrea Bocelli

My soul wept while you sang,
my soul trembled,
as your voice lifted it higher.
As you touched my core,
I became an infant,
I was a little girl running
toward my father's arms,
I was a woman loved.
All the moments unfolded into one,
a thousand yesterdays and today,
interwoven into a beautiful tapestry of my life.
My soul trembled,
touching dark places
where now there is light,
reaching inside my spirit
to everything I ever was,
and all that I am.
Erase the past,
celebrate the past,
devastation replaced by triumph.
I wept as if I had wings,
lifting me over oceans and mountains
I have loved.
Completely captivated
in the moment,
yet I melted into
a thousand mournful mornings,
of despair and loneliness,
of judgment and courage.
A thousand moments
engraved in my being.
A thousand tangos I have danced while I stood still.
All the while,
my soul weeping,

the scars cracked,
open and bleeding.
My soul weeping with the grace of knowing,
that the pages are full,
that I have lived,
that I have loved,
that we are here
for a moment in time.
We blink and the
here and now
are gone.

The Stillness

The seed sprouts into a plant,
dawn turns into a new day,
the infant grows,
and so did our love.
I did not ask you for eternity,
I did not seek, question,
judge,
I did not rush your love.
I took it one day at a time,
one stolen kiss,
one moment of desire,
drops of magic in the sands of time.
In the stillness of dawn
our love is sacred.
You reach for me,
our tangled feet meet,
the silence cradles us in the moment.
There are no interruptions,
or decisions to make,
or small stuff to sweat,
or words we may utter and regret.
In the stillness of dawn,
love is reborn,
like the new day.
All that was said is forgotten
and forgiven
in the stillness of dawn
we remember
how we became one.

My Tree

The veins in my hands deep, pronounced,
like the roots of the oak tree, strong and enduring.
My crow's feet light
but aged,
like the cracks in the tree seasoned and broken down.
On the doorstep of spring
the bark peels without warning.
On the doorstep of spring,
my soul is fractured
from the crevices of life.
My inner bark is living
forming new protective layers.
We both weathered life,
at times, beaten and broken,
yet we are both survivors.
New twigs are forming,
green leaves are sprouting,
and I am growing new stems to extend,
to uncover and remedy
doubt and fear.
My spirit soars higher
than my body can.
It struggles
to follow the questions,
to explore the possibilities,
to provoke,
to seek.
When you look into my eyes
can you see the stains on my soul?
I bow my head
and
then I rise
like the roots of the oak tree soaking it all in,
loving life.

Joshua

I've been told that my face lights up
when I see you.
What they can not see is that
my heart dances,
and soars.
The sun seeped into my soul
the day you were born,
wrinkled skin,
ten fingers,
ten toes,
my spirit bloomed.
You smiled and
touched my face,
I felt pure love and devotion.
Time stood still,
as I held you,
my heart full.
We grew side by side,
two peas in a pod, bookends.
Life was messy, imperfect,
but I stood in the storm,
faced the dragons,
looked them in the eye,
and looked within my soul.
I nourished you with love,
I nourished you with books,
words danced between us.
The pages of our life filled
with wonder and discoveries.
Delightful things you said
filled with wisdom, and tenderness
as I listened in awe.
You taught me forgiveness and redemption.
I taught you that the world

was yours,
to listen to your heart
and extend your gifts to the world.
Compassion and love,
one life,
one step at a time.
There was a time I carried you
in my arms,
your legs wrapped around my waist.
Now,
I carry you in my heart,
in every thought,
in every waking moment.
I love you forever my son.

My Snow Angel

You made snow angels
in the white soft snow.
The sun was honey colored,
like the color of my dreams.
The moments fleeting,
it was not lost on me.
I knew that these are magical moments that
will become a rarity,
because I gave you wings
to soar up high,
to fly,
to taste freedom and life.
I savored the hours,
through my dark glasses.
My soul rested,
the way we did in the lodge
up in the woods.
Snow was silent,
like my thoughts.
I left the worries behind,
to elevate my soul,
to lay my weary heart
in a safe place.
I listened to the mountains
as the sun rose
it brushed up against them
and fondled them.
I drank coffee in front of the fire,
I listened to the woods,
I listened to my spirit.
Now,
the tree is twinkling,
your baby ornaments wink attempting
to make me smile.

My dreams came true,
you created a life
you soar like the stars,
This Christmas my heart will
miss you more than you'll ever know.

Gratitude

Words on trees
pretending to be leaves,
swaying in the breeze,
floating in the universe.
Kindness,
hope,
inspiration,
love,
grace,
faith,
peace,
words to live by.
I choose you, gratitude,
to be the one for me.
Gratitude,
you whisper in my ear,
when I awaken from my sleep.
I hear your voice
in my dreams.
I have walked with you,
through our long journey.
You found me in a dark place,
and you lifted me,
you pulled thorns out of my soul.
We choose words,
to walk with them,
a word to define the year,
to define intention.
A new day,
a new page,
we slice to pieces,
to savor,
to squander away.

We choose a word to stuff
into the pockets of our hearts,
to fly on the wings of our spirit.
Gratitude,
you are my constant companion.
I whisper your
name a thousand times.
I dance with you in the rain,
you embrace me when I weep.
You are simple and complicated,
you are fear,
you are love.
You are tears,
you are laughter.
I carry you as
you carry me.

Happy Thirteenth Daniel

Cinnamon the bear
lay on my bed,
where you left him to shelter me
and keep me company
while I was sick.
He was wearing his yellow and white bowtie
which made me think of springtime,
and how you love me
like the stars that map the sky,
and the moon that peeks through your window
playing hide and seek,
like the night light when you were small
and proudly you said the word moon
for the first time.
Your golden locks were soft,
and your sweet smile
seeped into my heart
while I welcomed your spirit.
Now you are older
you read my words,
and you understand.
You find love in my poetry
and in between the lines
all the while listening to my heart.
It seems like yesterday,
it seems like long ago,
when you entered my world,
your eyes alert
with a twinkle like no other.
I love your laughter,
giggles,
idiosyncrasies.
I love that you ponder

the big questions of life
and the small ones.
I love that you are a boy that thinks
about heaven
and if we go there
and the meaning of our existence.
At the same time
I love
that you explore
how fast to solve
the Rubik's cube,
and that
you design virtual worlds.
I love your conversation and animation.
I love that you are gentle and kind,
and that you reside in an old soul.
I love your vocab and grammar,
enthusiasm and wonder.
I love that you are proper
and that you savor life while
you soak it all in.
You are my light,
my inspiration,
I love you forevermore.

She Will Be on the Moon

If you love the poet,
you must read her words,
so you can feel her soul
and listen to her heart.
You will find her on the moon,
dangling on a vine
smelling roses,
and chasing butterflies.
You must know her love is true,
and her passion is fierce.
Her gypsy eyes will
tell you all that you need to know.
She will write poetry on your skin,
and cradle you through the night.
She has made amends,
and created dreams.
She has flowers blooming in her heart,
and wisdom seeds she keeps
in her soul from all the pain and joy.
When you love the poet,
you must read her words,
so you can touch her soul,
and capture her essence.

Gratitude of a Wounded Soul

A wounded soul
has danced a thousand tangos,
in ballrooms under the stars
and in gutters under an
orange and crimson sky.
A wounded soul
has wept a thousand tears,
swords and spears
punctured and pierced
its spirit,
it has nursed cuts
and healed scars
along the way.
A wounded soul is kind
from surviving the battle.
A wounded soul comes from
a place where sorrow lived.
It does not know fear for itself but it feels it for others.
It knows hunger and pain, solitude and abandonment.
It knows forgiveness,
and loss in an intimate way.
A wounded soul sees beauty, and possesses it deep within.
A wounded soul knows gratitude,
it knows what drowning feels like while gasping for a breath of
air.
A wounded soul knows gratitude for the sacred moments of
love and ordinary magic.
A wounded soul does not search for purpose,
it has one.
A wounded soul does not
let strangers define it,
it follows it's
inner compass,
with grace and glory.

My Wish

For Daniel

The vultures stood tall on the clock tower,
looking ominous on that gray rainy day.
I wondered who had
they come for.
Had they come for me,
was it time for
confession and redemption.
Was it time for the soul
to be naked and exposed.
I'm not afraid to die,
there's an army of angels waiting for me,
holding lanterns in the dark,
 shining a light through the path of eternity.
I'm not afraid to die,
but I am afraid to leave you.
I'm afraid your soul
will saturate
with pain
and that your laughter will cease.
I fear that my arms
won't stretch long enough
for you to feel my embrace.
I fear that you would think
I left you,
that I failed you.
I'm not afraid to die,
but I fear that no one
will love you the way I do.
I wish for you to live,
I ask you to inhale the universe,
and be one with it.
Peel the layers of life

and taste the sweet nectar.
Skip through the stars,
and rejoice in every small miracle that disguises itself as
ordinary.
I wish for you to awaken your senses
and open your heart,
that is what I wish for you
my love.

Grace

Grace is found in the ocean,
on waves full of purpose and intention,
waves that linger like an old memory
leaving salt on our skin.
Grace is found in confinement,
when light dances through shadows,
and hope drifts through the walls.
Grace is found when you've lost
your way in the universe, and
you find a lighthouse to guide your way.
Grace is found in nursing a bird with a broken wing
and watching it fly away.
Grace is found in a wildflower,
blooming on the side of a majestic mountain.
Grace is found in holding the hand of someone you love
while they take their last breath.
Grace is found in giving your heart completely
without reservation or hesitation.
Grace is found in the taste of coffee
when migraine robs you of your sleep,
and you are grateful
that you did not die
while fighting the battles of life,
and while you were wrestling with demons.
You learned hard lessons
when your hand was in the fire,
in the burn you
found truth,
you found courage,
you found grace.

A New Day

The moon illuminated the night,
ripe with glory,
brimming with truth.
I watched with longing as
I crawled away from dark places.
My stories shattered,
the melancholy soaking through
my bones.
My voice audible,
my hips wider,
my spirit soaring,
years of rage and silence,
despair and celebration.
The trees listened to my cries,
they whispered to me
their tales of sorrow and triumph.
Lessons learned from failure,
redemption answered by forgiveness.
The surroundings faded into a blur
immersed in what is present.
I rejoice in the sound of his breath
laying next to me,
swept away in sweet slumber.
He seeps hope into the storms of my soul.

9/11

For Kevin W. Donnelly and for Luciana
for being and sharing that moment.

I stand silent,
at first, a single tear rolls down my face.
My hand touches the bronze plates,
names inscribed.
My mind is silent,
my thoughts drowning
as the waterfalls cascade down.
A storm brewing within,
the tears are flowing.
An ache I buried,
rising to the surface.
The wound oozes,
it bleeds.
The sun is shining,
the wind on my face,
neither one comforts me,
nor ease my sorrow.
Stories told by loved ones,
about loss,
of lives gone too soon.
They will be remembered
their faces, and smiles,
their birthdays,
and the moments that
made up their lives.
I want to search for your name,
but I am told that I'll never find you.
An unexplainable feeling comes over me,
I am drawn
to glance away,
and there I find you,

your name in bold letters.
We never met,
but I was told you were
a gentle soul,
a hero,
a son,
a brother,
an uncle,
a boyfriend
a friend.
You were so many things to
so many people.
Your light illuminated their world.
Your name etched,
among your friends,
among heroes like you.
I stand silent,
drowning in the moment,
closing my eyes,
and feeling the pain sear within.

Dare to Dream

A green notebook
I bought in the Harvard bookstore,
rests in my pocket.
A notebook wallpapered with words
of triumph and despair,
of highs and lows,
of salvation and redemption.
I didn't dare to dream,
to study in a beautiful university
with beautiful
minds,
and manicured lawns that
I could rest my weary head on.
I didn't think I was good enough
or brave enough.
I was told that I was beautiful
more often than
I was told that I was smart.
I didn't dare to dream for me
but I did dream it for you.
I dreamt the sky was the limit,
and that you would sparkle in the universe.
You would learn
and you would grow.
My little boy,
you held a beating heart in your hand.
You saved a life today,
and yesterday.
You shine when you speak,
your actions filled with
compassion,
even when you are tired and weary,
you find the strength to help someone.

You don't seek recognition
or merit,
your reward is
the fulfillment you feel within.
I didn't dare to dream
for me
but I dared to dream for you.

Not Chasing Yesterday

I am standing still
in the moment.
I'm not chasing my youth,
I left it behind me.
I savor today,
I carry a lantern to light
my way through the walls
of my heart.
I possess a childish enthusiasm,
even though the road was rugged.
My sense of wonder
may be tainted, but
not diminished or broken.
The light in my eyes
at times filled
with darkness.
I remember pieces
of my childhood,
laughter and sadness.
A pin an astronaut gave me when I was six,
songs I sang with my dad on a worn out tape,
books holding the secrets of the world,
poems I wrote as a little girl,
in colorful dog eared notebooks.
Dots on a map of a life
well lived.
I have savored sweetness,
and swam in melancholy,
I have climbed over
walls that imprisoned me,
I have confronted what was expected
of me,
and I chose my own path,
my own way.

I chewed those moments
without regret.
I don't want yesterday's
leftovers,
I don't wish to recycle my dreams.
No,
I have grown,
changed,
evolved.
I'm not chasing yesterday,
I am living today.

I Know Love

Love,
I know you,
like the first sentence in a
poem I walk into.
Love,
I know you like a wave in the ocean washing over me,
like the wind in my hair,
like mom's baking.
Love
I know you,
like the breath I inhale,
like a song I hum,
like the sand on my feet,
like a dream I had
last night.
Love,
I know you,
like Sunday,
like a sunrise on vacation,
like the taste of my childhood.
Love,
I know you,
like homecoming,
like rolling in the mud,
like banana ice cream,
like lemon,
unmistakable,
distinct, irreplaceable, defined.
My love fierce,
my love eternal,
my love yours completely.

Murky Waters

Confessions of the soul
take place on dark alleyways,
and on sunny open fields
of green.
If I open my heart
would you still love me?
Will you still throw bouquets at my feet,
and give me accolades.
Would you deem me insane for wanting to die?
Would you deem me insane for wanting to live?

The past resides within,
it is my companion.
I threw myself into murky waters
without knowing how to swim.
I learned lessons while
I was drowning.
Confessions of the soul,
we carry them like fragile threads that come undone.
The anchor within releases,
we let them go,
finding ourselves free.

The Past

Ice cube under my tongue,
I close my eyes
not to savor
but to remember.
Ice cubes filled my belly,
drowning the sound of hunger.
Isolation,
thoughts unraveled,
like threads undone.
Shackled by yesterday
a prisoner of the past.
Searing pain,
I close my eyes to remember.

Honeysuckle Summer

Love poems tucked away
in your tackle box.
Love poems engraved on your skin.
At dawn, the house exhales,
as I inhale your breath.
You walk through fire with me,
you dance through the storm with me.
You give me honeysuckle in an empty Coca Cola bottle,
just like that summer in the Hamptons long ago.
You whispered tales
and secrets of your childhood
enchanted summers you had.
I marveled at the stained glass windows
on the charming little church down the road,
by the graveyard.
The sun nurtured us
and caressed our bare skin,
and yellow flowers in
an empty soda can
were a gift I treasured
because you loved me.

Jacob

Your spirit will live in the woods,
running wild and free.
Your spirit will dance through
the Sequoia trees.
Your spirit will shine
brightest among the stars.
Your spirit will frolic in
the waves of the ocean.
Your spirit will live in
the house you dwelt in
with your soul mate.
Your spirit will live in your daughter's eyes.
Your spirit will live in green vineyards
under a turquoise sky.
Your spirit will live in vibrant
flowers blooming in the spring.
Your spirit will live in
everyone you touched,
your soul soaring high.
Goodbye my friend,
until we meet again.

Lessons

Your fears melted like snow,
you confessed
your father's sins,
knowing they were not yours
to absolve.
His sins were not your
burden to carry.
You held your head high
and marched into the world.
I had wished that I
possessed your courage,
I wished that I was brave like you.
You let out the secrets,
ripples in the pond of life,
scattered like confetti in the wind,
pieces of our life.
Vulnerable you ignored,
the judgment of others.
You gave me strength to blossom,
wings to carry me home,
you made my burden lighter.
I watched your fortitude,
and I knew then,
that the fears were never yours but mine.

On This Day

I love the loud jovial voices
carried on the waters in the bay
on a summer day.
When the sun is caressing our bare skin,
and the light is dancing in a festive celebration.
In those moments
I don't question life,
or life's meaning.
In those moments
I feel it in my marrow,
unspoken,
throbbing,
clear.
I watch smiling children
and I laugh as they play
with dogs with sweet faces.
I know the meaning of life,
I may question it on another day,
I may ponder,
but not on this day.
I taste salt on my lover's skin
and I ache for more.
I breathe in the ocean air.
I feel alive,
I know I have arrived at my destination.
The hunger in my soul,
moans less,
because I feel a little fuller.

For Mom

On Mother's Day,
flowers will be given,
hallmark cards will be read,
children will make breakfast for moms well deserved.
I will think of you,
under the sand,
under the stone we erected,
announcing to the world that
you were a great wife,
mother,
grandmother,
great grandmother.
A trophy for all your sleepless nights,
and heartache.
I placed a heart
shaped stone,
in your grave
before they covered you.
I cried, my heart broken.
Life is fleeting you said,
surround yourself with beauty you said.
You gave love with warm kisses,
and embraces,
sweet words you spoke.
You were flawed,
but beautiful.
Fragile but powerful.
I believed in miracles,
I believed that you would go on,
that you would overcome the heartbreak,
of losing the love of your life.
In the rehab room,
you saw him even though he was gone,
you saw him smile.

You no longer cared about life,
I tried to awaken your spirit but
your eyes were vacant
with only endless sadness
that invaded your being.
He was your other half,
he was your life.
I saw you wither,
I saw you disappear in front of me.
I fed you orange pudding,
the way you fed me when I was a child.
You followed me with your eyes,
but you no longer smiled,
the stars had disappeared from them.
You melted into the bed,
and my words could not move you nor lift your spirit.
I didn't want to let you go,
I didn't want to say goodbye.
When you took your last breath,
my heart stopped,
my pain raw and unbearable.
I hold you in my heart,
I wear the wedding ring my father gave you,
I hold you in my dreams,
and every day I think of you,
longing,
always longing.

Watching from Heaven

Dad,
you would have given me the moon
if you could,
lasso it down and hold it in
your palm to light my way.
You told me tales of horses with
broken spirits,
knowing that mine was one.
You kissed me goodnight thousands
of nights always telling me that you loved me.
You inspired me,
believed in me,
forgave me.
You delighted in my words,
encouraged my abstract thoughts.
You were a giant of a man,
you were always there.
Dad,
I wish I could find the small Italian restaurant,
in London
on the side street by the Thames river.
The sounds of the city were left outside,
wet we took refuge
from the rain.
We feasted on pasta and roasted chicken,
as if we climbed into one of the
Botticelli paintings we saw that day.
Warm, the colors lifting our spirits.
We were delighted in the moment
and a day filled with beauty.
I want to walk into the past,
and find you there in spirit.
I want to replay our conversation,
the sights and sounds.

I want to sit down
with my dog eared notebook,
and write poetry that you would love,
poetry that you can see from heaven.
Dad,
you loved London,
she seeped into your heart
and claimed it.
You repeated a quote,
"when a man is tired of London,
he is tired of life,"
it resonated in your soul,
because to you she felt like home.
I want to go to her ,
and breathe her in again,
and feel you walk beside me.
I want to go to her,
and find you there in spirit
and know that you are still watching me
from where you are in heaven.

Boston Strong

Morning dawns
with a new promise.
He stretches in his sleep,
as I watch the rain
dancing on my window.
I inhale coffee from a tall cup.
I wake him with a gentle touch
and tender words.
A week ago,
the world shattered for so many.
He has watched and listened
to images of terror,
sadness seeping into his big
brown eyes.
He felt compassion for
the lives lost,
for the lives injured.
He felt pride that his brother
is a doctor in this wonderful city.
A week ago our world changed,
the rhythm of the city silenced,
our flags pressed against our chest.
Our land sighed,
our land ached.
We remember the victims,
smiling from old photographs.
Children kneeling by a candlelight vigil,
mothers holding hands tighter.
We remember the injured,
runners shoes and messages
hung by Boylston Street.
We are broken yet strong,
hurt but not defeated.
I hold my son,

I whisper words about goodness,
dark moments that inspire light.
I hold him closer and give him wings of hope and love,
wanting my words to shelter him from the storm,
wanting them to lift his soul.

Our Garden, Our Change

We choose our battles,
our garden filled with weeds and thorns.
We plant seeds and wait for
the branches of our heart to soar higher.
Outside the walls of our mind
we embrace the truth.
The streets are like old silver,
full of tarnished dreams.
Let the dreams find the way,
let the soul reach the sky as
we tackle the battles in our yard,
our home,
knowing that we can change our demons.
We can transform,
we can evolve.
We can not sweep mistakes,
the way we rake leaves,
but we can wear them proudly,
like a crown of flowers
from our garden.

Feed the Soul

If you were the one to birth words,
I would make you a garden
to plant them in.
I would water them,
nurture them,
and watch them grow.
If you wrote words on my skin,
I would undress in the ocean,
I would read them out loud
and let the waves wash
them off my canvas,
and carry them away in the outgoing tide.
If words were your passion,
I would gather them in my pockets,
and keep them safe in a locket
by my heart.
I would guard them for you
until you would release them,
and let them fly
into the universe.
Ink drops written with your blood,
words saturated with
reason and madness,
sorrow and joy,
words that feed the soul.

Happy Valentine

Valentine,
your breath on mine,
sweet escape,
you fill the pages of my heart.
Gentle when you touch my soul,
you shake my spirit with yours.
Valentine,
you are Sunday,
you are the stars on a Key West night,
you are the cathedral of Muir Woods.
Valentine,
will you still love me
when my mermaid's hair turns white.
Will you still love me when my eyes
stop shining like the stars in the evening sky.
Will you still love me when I am frail and weak,
will you love me for all time,
even if I lose my mind,
even if I no longer know your name,
and no longer recognize the sound of your voice.
Valentine,
will you be there for me to lean on,
to warm my days with new memories,
to make your laughter my new soundtrack,
will you be my everything,
will you love me for all time?

Super Bowl XLVII

New Orleans caressed us with her eyelashes,
inspired us to dream of
things we can't see or touch.
We walked her streets feeling her,
charming buildings,
with cast iron balconies,
a melting pot,
a home of great writers,
you can feel the spirits of the past,
loud in the present moment.
Colorful people,
colorful beads.
I've had my share of cafe au lait,
with beignets,
at Cafe Du Monde.
I have listened to tales
with my heart open.
New Orleans,
intimate like an old friend,
you visit,
delightful like a new one.
That was years ago,
but never forgotten,
only stored in the attics of my mind
for safekeeping.
Today we reminisce,
today,
game day
we wait with anticipation.
Sinful foods and drinks ,
and laughter
in the house.
On the field,
festivities unfold,

the Armed Forces Color Guard presents the flags.
Our hearts beat like their drums.
The broadcast takes us to Afghanistan,
true heroes watching with pride.
They sacrifice,
so we can be free,
so we can play this game.
"America the Beautiful"
Sandy Hook Elementary Chorus,
brings us to tears.
The Star Spangled Banner is
sung beautifully on the field.
We are overcome by emotion,
we weep.
Ravens or 49ers,
I have listened to their stories
and their struggles.
The road challenging,
stepping stones,
that brought them here,
there are no losers today.
The highs and lows of today
will forever be imprinted on their hearts.
Today a celebration for
them,
for us and
for freedom.

My Beloved

You traced a heart on the shower door,
a love letter to me.
The water fell
the way the rain did on the roof
of our summer refuge.
I traced my fingers on your skin,
words of love,
poetry I long to give you.
Your wings carry me,
your branches embrace me.
You are my ocean,
you are my home.
Your passion fierce as the wind,
your love tender.
I love your imperfections.
I love the fire in your eyes.
I love your mischief,
always a boy,
yet a strong man.
Five A.M,
we inhale coffee,
our feet tangled together.
Waiting for our day to begin,
a new page to fill.

Happy Birthday Josh—2013

Your eyes shine,
like lanterns in the dark,
illuminating my soul.
The day you were born,
I knew my heart would never be the same.
My soul sang,
I found home.
I paint the sky,
I reach for the stars,
it's your birthday.
The canvas of our life,
abstract, vibrant with color.
We have grown,
through tears and laughter, curve-balls and hurdles.
We weathered,
high tides,
low tides,
pulling a red wagon
filled with dreams.
I wish your road is lighter .
I wish your life is filled with wonder.
I wish you love,
every day of your life.
Your eyes humble,
you have not learned
to embrace how great you are.
I knew all along,
your noble heart,
your healing hands,
carry the strength of your spirit.
Your soul dancing,
majestic,
beautiful.

Son, I look into your eyes,
you are the right I have done
in this world.
My love infinite,
swept in awe,
my baby boy,
you grew into a great man.
Happy birthday, my love.

History Unfolds—2013

His head rests on me,
I touch his hair,
soft and wild.
He looks at me from the corner of
his eye.
He is wearing his, "I love Bacon" shirt.
We watch the inauguration,
he rolls into a pretzel next to me.
Twelve years old and restless.
I want him to witness
this moment in time.
Lives sacrificed so
we can be free.
Mothers, fathers, sisters,
brothers, children,
are all present in this crowd.
A sea of humanity,
all anticipating this moment.
Pride within them,
the blood in their veins,
red, white and blue.
He groans, half yawning,
hoping I let him go back to his room.
I hope he takes this in,
it's a part of him,
a part of us.
I tell him he is blessed
and privileged,
to be born under these blue skies,
where he is free.
Where his voice is heard,
where he counts.
America

I have laid my head
on your chest,
and I listened to your heartbeat.
America
you brought me to my knees,
poured salt in my wounds and healed me.
You lifted me,
you embraced me,
you gave me a home.

Home for Christmas

He hovers as I sleep,
waiting for me to open my eyes and smile.
I rub the sleep out of my eyes,
sensing his anticipation.
Christmas morning feels magical,
Elvis singing Christmas songs,
while we inhale coffee.
Snow globes shining,
lights twinkling,
hearts dancing as one.
He wants to wake his brother up,
but he has to wait until nine o'clock.
My thoughts wander to
children abandoned and abused
in shelters plucked away from family,
they have no safe place.
A man I met the other day
finds hope in every child,
and dedicates his life to helping them.
He traded his chain to buy his wife
a ring for Christmas.
He left the corporate world,
for a job at the shelter.
The job doesn't pay much
but he is richer than many people
that I know.
His eyes light up as he shares
his heart with me.
My heart rejoices because I know
our paths crossed for a reason.
My little one urges again,
and my thoughts wander back.

After the gifts,
after breakfast,
we watch television
by the tree.
The tree breathes with us,
as we breathe with gratitude.

I Live

I live
again these days.
Don't think I have forgotten you,
my thoughts find you in the alleyways
of my mind.
Early dawn,
the house is dark and quiet
I awaken thinking of you.
Fragments of dreams,
left behind.
I search through mingled trees,
and dark forests.
I search for you.
These days,
I laugh,
something I had forgotten to do.
I catch a glimpse of my old self,
the sadness melting from my eyes.
I remember the passion you had
for life.
I remember lessons taught by example.
Yesterday I was but a shadow of myself,
today I step into my body
and reclaim my soul.
I heal my broken stems,
I grow new leaves.
I walk among the starfish,
I skip among the stars.
I fly
because you taught me that I can.
I fly
because one day we will meet again.
These days,
I live again.
Don't think I have forgotten.

The Journey

For Josh and Daniel

We walk,
our steps rushed,
the ground hard.
The sun is shy but
smiles upon us.
I ignore the wind,
playing with my hair.
I am listening closely,
to you speaking,
kindly,
softly,
trying to heal the bruised ego of your brother.
His tears cascading down,
his exam a disappointment.
You carry his heavy backpack,
wanting to lighten his burden.
I listen as you encourage,
with words of tenderness.
His glasses fog up,
from tears and distress.
You hand him a napkin to wipe
them away.
My boys,
one a man,
the other still a child.
Your story weaved with love.
The beauty of the moment cherished in my mind.
On the way to the airport,
bumper to bumper traffic.
We take side streets,
as our afternoon unfolds.
I will savor today,

the snapshot of my sons,
standing side by side.
I will soak it in,
with grace and gratitude in my heart.

A Moment of Life

In the corner of the room,
the green dragon watches silently.
He stands tall,
wrapped around the spear from Kung Fu.
His older brother left it as a joke,
like a note trail
reminding him that he was there.
I watch him as he writes an essay
about uniforms stifling individuality,
his eyes intense,
his fingers flying on the keyboard.
The book he read on Tesla
on the nightstand,
along with twenty-five dollars,
he earned folding laundry.
His effort toward raising
money for Thanksgiving baskets for
the less fortunate.
His father walks in
to listen to the essay.
I inhale the moment in this room,
painted with blue walls,
SpongeBob bedsheets,
and a bunny he still tucks
under his arm in his sleep.
The bunny battles nightmares,
and keeps this space safe.
My boy,
his eyes sparkle ,
his imagination bigger than these walls.
His imagination takes flight,
and has no limits.
I watch with tenderness.

Promises Kept

Colorful Lego bricks scattered
like confetti on the ground.
Spaceships and rockets built,
a feast to my eyes.
His eyes shine as he runs to me,
"I need electrical parts for my Legos."
I smile quietly,
"please mom"
his voice urges.
I take a deep breath.
"We will see, " I answer.
My thoughts unravel,
as he chatters away,
details of inventions and
dreams he dreams.
He captures my attention with
his enthusiasm.
An ache fills me,
as I watch him build a fort
out of food cans,
I want to shield his heart.
I have to make up for a dad
that's not present in his life.
I have to make up for promises
his dad did not keep,
a treehouse he said he would build,
baseball he said he would play,
but he did not,
tears of a little boy.
I need to fix it with a band-aid to his soul,
he is five and I am twenty-nine.
We are growing and learning together.

I hold him closer,
shelter him from the pain,
nourish him with books and love.
I remain silent,
and determined,
I never make a promise that I can't keep.

The Fourth Floor

For Safta Dora

Grandma lived on the fourth floor,
but you would never know it.
A jungle of
plants adorning her terrace,
serenity would wash over us when we were small.
We could see the zoo from the terrace,
we would spy on the giraffes,
the smell would rise above on windy days.
That was before developers came in and bought the land.
I missed the zoo when it closed down,
the feeling I was in a faraway place,
even though I was caged in the city.
Grandma had open arms,
and an open heart.
Her kitchen abundant with food,
cooked with love.
She was sunny,
and colorful like the beads she wore.
Her eyes blue as the ocean,
her strength deep,
but silent.
She had wisdom that was not taught in books,
but in living life.
Grandma smiled with kindness, as
she offered cassata ice cream,
three flavors living side by side,
in a box of wonder.
Her eyes would sparkle,
as we tasted the sweetness.
She had endured war and loss,
unimaginable pain.

Yet, she found the way,
her days unfolding,
her days filled with simple gratitude.
Her ways taught us,
about love and family,
about dignity,
and survival.
Grandma lived on the fourth floor,
you would never know it because it was a world of its own.

True to Myself

Grief tastes like bitter tea leaves,
floating in sewer water.
Grief tastes like limoncello
I drank when my dad died.
In my head the silence is loud,
screaming, roaring.
On other days, the noise is silent, gagged,
still.
This invisible bubble between us,
I don't want to swim in these waters
filled with misery.
Falling into grief,
I am grateful, but
I am human and I am flawed.
I need to feel the storm sweeping
me away inside my thoughts,
leaving an imprint on my spirit.
I need to stand still and acknowledge it,
and welcome it,
I need to feel it sear my soul.
I do not mean to cause you more pain,
I do not mean to linger,
I just need to be true to myself.
I remember when my mom was sick,
and dying,
I came to you depleted,
you held me,
our eyes interlocked,
I inhaled your breath as you inhaled my sorrow.
We've been here before,
this part of life,
facing that we have no control.

Life is fragile,
pain is pain,
and there is no sequel.
I do not mean to cause you any pain,
I do not mean to linger,
I just need to be true to myself.

Forever Daisy

By the gates of heaven, you'll wait for me,
wagging your tail in delight and
howling to greet me,
and I will smile.
By the gates of heaven, you'll wait for me,
the way you waited every day
for me to return home,
celebrating my arrival,
your happiness innocent,
and unbridled.
I see you in every corner,
in every step I walk alone.
I celebrate sun-kissed days
we had,
a life shared,
sweet memories that live in my heart.
By the gates of heaven,
I will lay down beside you,
and roll with you among the clouds.
I will hold you,
the way I held you in my arms today,
when we said goodbye.
Until then,
swim in aquamarine pools,
run in sunflower fields
chasing lizards and butterflies.
Run through the fields of heaven,
until we meet once again.

Truth

We die slowly every day,
we juggle our days,
spinning our hours away,
moments of epiphany,
moments of despair,
on autopilot.
Hours laced with routine and responsibilities,
while we bury our desires.
Dentist appointments,
grocery shopping, playdates.
I hunt for a tomato,
I smell one and then another,
until I smell one with sweet aroma.
I close my eyes and wonder.
We juggle while we wish to save the world,
save the dolphins,
save the oceans,
save ourselves.
We die a little more,
holes in our hearts,
emptiness we cannot fill,
band-aids to social issues we can't solve.
We strive to save the world,
while we die a little more.
The game room at the pediatric dentist office
diverts the children with electronic games.
Mothers distracted on their iPhone.
Down the road, five miles away,
there are hungry
children that come to school with empty bellies.
Hungry for the free lunch,
that will sustain them for another day.
We die a little every day.

Small Bites

The city is buzzing,
a man wearing a hat walks by with his dog.
A little boy and his grandma find shade,
under a tree in front of the Modern Museum of Art.
An ambulance screaming,
the city boisterous.
I take it in,
poetic colorful streets.
I find serenity at the outside garden cafe,
at the museum,
while nursing a Diet Coke,
and dark chocolate ice cream,
calling the people I love.
My boy is sleeping,
recovering from the night shift.
I wait to cook for him,
a homemade meal,
made with love,
and embrace him and his overgrown beard.
I escape for a day or two,
I don't want to wait for my dreams,
I want to live them in
small delicious bites.
A night earlier, at Fenway Park,
Americana at it's best,
The Red Sox vs. The Yankees,
on a hot September night.
We reminisce about baseball games,
we went to when he was a child.
Games with extra innings,
caught in the rain, wet from head to toe.
I laugh because my heart is full.
I laugh because my boy has grown
into a fine man.

Forgiveness

Butterflies in my hair,
butterflies in my head,
thoughts born to take flight.
In a Chinese restaurant in San Francisco,
I thought of you.
Tables in booths with curtains drawn,
in my mind like confessionals at church.
A small cubicle,
with an unspoken promise.
You spill your soul hoping for a new slate,
a new day.
The soul waiting absolution.
The soul delights as it rises
through green fields of forgiveness.
All of us sinners,
with our poison of choice,
our path muddy,
on our journey.
Sins fester inside,
imprisoned in our being.
We bury them without allowing
them wings to fly,
we watch our dreams die,
leaving them in a bottomless ocean of pain.

Walk with Me
Boston Holocaust Museum

Walk with me
among my people,
their lives were lost,
their innocence was stolen,
their futures were robbed.
Walk with me
among these glass towers,
engraved with numbers.
These numbers represent them,
steam rising through metal grates,
my insides turning inside out.
Tears falling for those slaughtered,
their voices silenced forever.
I feel one with them.
I am one with them.
I stand silently and,
I read quotes inscribed of survivors left behind.
My heart saturated with pain.
Images seared in my mind.
of people dying,
families vanished,
children that will never grow up.
My great grandparents,
their home burnt to the ground,
murdered in cold blood.
My heart heavy,
I want you to walk with me,
through the gates of hell,
where humanity lost its mind,
where humanity lost itself.
Stand beside me,
hold my hand,

feel my beating heart,
screaming in rage.
My veins filled with legacy of persecution,
honor,
and pain.
Walk with me as one,
feel my soul sigh in anguish.
Remember those silenced,
remember the past,
and let it never happen again.

Goodbye

For Sieg

Soft currents,
rough waves,
sadness floats through aquamarine waters.
Not long ago
we dipped in the cold ocean,
collecting shells,
talking about life and death,
blond little boys you loved,
that captured your heart,
adventures we stumbled on,
books that we read.
We left footprints on the sand
as we shared food and laughter,
tales of fish caught,
tears of loss.
We escaped the rainstorm that day,
not knowing that it will be the last time
we would share these waters.
Goodbye my friend,
sleep with the angels.
May your spirit soar,
may you find peace,
you will be missed.

Jayden

Her golden hair,
bounces softly.
Her eyes are fields of green.
She holds my hand,
she wants to show me the night sky.
The dream catcher hanging on her window,
catches nightmares,
and carries them away from this room filled with love.
This room filled with stars she sees
in her chandelier
and princess Barbie dolls
that comfort her,
and whisper tales in her ear.
She plays with my hair
and I laugh
because her small hands feel
like waves in the ocean
comforting and dreamy.
I laugh because her words are tender,
and her heart is open.
Her eyes sparkle as she calls me
Aunt Sushi,
instead of Aunt Mushy
and we giggle.
Her laugh infectious,
the sound of sweetness.
We read a book about the Statue of Liberty,
it took 214 crates to bring her to America.
We read a book about Abe Lincoln,
and how he stuffed notes in his hat.
We pretend to be mermaids in the ocean,
while she tells me she loves purple and red.
She rests her head on my shoulder.

She holds me for a moment,
and captures my heart.
Jayden,
her eyes full of dreams,
her mind filled with imagination,
her heart full of love.

Invisible Heroes

Heat rises from the streets,
sounds heard,
a cell phone in the distance,
an ambulance siren,
all in the shadows of the white,
pristine stadium along Biscayne Bay.
Million dollar condos on the waterfront,
larger than life portraits,
of the basketball home town heroes,
painted on the facade of the stadium.
The avenue glowing like
a pregnant woman in
her glory.
A walk away,
the opposite avenue, dying a slow death.
Smell of urine and semen rising
from the street.
The sad reality of brothers
living on cardboard boxes
on the pavement.
Drivers passing by,
afraid to look into their eyes.
Brothers that once bled
red, white, and blue
in unforgiving foreign green fields.
Long before America
led parades for heroes.
Long before small children
waved their flags in welcome.
In those days,
warriors were neglected,
set aside,
disposed of.

Parades were canceled and revoked,
real heroes fighting for our freedom,
No larger than life portraits
painted for them.

An Empty Chair for Mom

There's an empty chair
beside me.
There's an empty place that only you can fill.
Yesterday's memories live
in the attic of my heart.
In a place that only you can reach and comfort.
I remain with
words you left behind,
love you gently carried,
postcards of places we've been to,
photographs of moments
of a life well lived.
I have drowned in sorrow,
I have lost my way.
I have carried a scar with your name.
Today
I want to dance in the rain,
and celebrate you.
I want to voice my gratitude to the world.
I want to bottle my tears
and save them for another day.
I want the wind to whistle secrets
in my ear.
Today I will soar and fly,
today I will live,
today I will celebrate you.

The Magic That Was You

For Mom

I inhale the peaches,
red and orange in color.
Peaches so perfect,
as if they escaped a Renoir painting.
I seek a bruised one,
and I delight that it's flawed.
I wait with anticipation
to slice into it.
I remember you,
gently holding a knife
and cutting into it.
A smile would appear
in the corners of your mouth,
when you tasted the sweetness.
I take a peach to my lips,
the taste almost intoxicating.
I wish I could share it with you, mom,
the way we shared so much.
I carried slices of pain,
between mother and daughter.
I held bitterness to unkind words,
unimportant and trivial.
Now that you're gone,
I have not forgotten,
the magic that you carried.
Love you scattered.
Your arms that like a blanket,
covered us and kept us warm.
The love that made walls into
a home.

I wish you knew,
that I miss you every day
since you have left.
When you enter my dreams,
I attempt to remember
fragments of you.
I remain longing for you,
for words I did not say,
those last few days.
You tried to speak
but I could not understand,
your tongue swollen,
your eyes desperate to reach me.
I hid the tears away but
you saw the undeniable pain in my eyes.
Mom, as I inhale this peach,
as I savor it,
I remember.
The longing lingers,
the pain remains
and I wish that you were here.

Boston—His City

I fall in love the minute we land.
Her skies grey,
yet they welcome me.
I take a deep breath,
I feel like I am home,
even though we just met.
She is his city
and so I feel like she's mine.
Her beauty unfolds as I
watch her awaken from her sleep.
I want to embrace her,
the way she embraces him.
I fall into her,
she is magical at sunrise
over the Boston harbor.
Red brick buildings,
historical walks,
ducks that come to life in a children's book,
that I read to him when he was a child.
In her streets I walk
feeling alive,
they tease me because my smile is wider,
my voice is lighter,
they don't understand that I am home.

Moments of Our Life

We stumble into Dunkin Donuts
with a desire for a good cup of Joe.
He cracks a joke with
the girls behind the counter,
and they smile, their day
becomes a little sunnier.
We eat breakfast sandwiches,
I watch the faces of those I love,
rubbing sleep from their eyes.
A good feeling washing over me.
We converse on the way to Cape Cod,
admiring small whimsical buildings,
American flags flying in the wind.
We stop at
a memorial for Kennedy and the Korean war,
I'm proud to be an American.
Unlike my children that were born into it,
I don't take it for granted.
I feel privileged,
a fire burning inside of me.
We find a restaurant that won
the best clam chowder
twelve times in a row.
Everyone is chatting
while waiting.
My love is like a little boy
as he tastes his childhood
in fried clams.
He smiles and voices gratitude
that we can
and so many can't.
At that moment I love him all over again,
I love them,
I love him,
my moment complete.

Words I Have Forgotten

I traced words on leaves,
with my fingers and my toes.
I scattered them in the orange grove,
and watched how they were swept into the heavens.
The fields nearby were Peridot green,
inviting and unassuming,
I knelt down,
wishing the scars would heal,
and I can find them once again.
The sun shined with regret,
attempting to console my emptiness.
The wounds of life led me to abandon
the words I love as I buried them deep inside.
Poetry, my old friend,
you found me while I played hide and seek
with my words.
While I wrote them on napkins and receipts
and tossed them away.
Poetry you found me in the ocean,
on a moonlit night,
the tide was rising,
the fish were biting.
You found me and I could no longer hide.
I had forgotten how you heal me,
how you awaken my desire,
how you let my soul dance outside my body.

His Life

Eleven o'clock
rolls around.
I watched the digital clock
countless times,
as I folded laundry and made the bed.
He gets off the night shift depleted,
and if he calls his voice is stuffed with fatigue.
He murmurs,
I can't understand
over the sounds of the city
coming through the phone.
Scattered words
about privacy laws,
and why he can't share information
about his patients.
I fish for details,
that never come.
Attempting to connect
the dots of his new life.
I walk on eggshells,
making small conversation,
when in reality I have so much to say.
I hold my breath,
because I no longer can fix his world.
I try to mend it but the world is cruel
in a way that even I can't understand,
because he won't let me in.
He won't turn on the light,
guarding the wall,
sheltering his sick patients and
their lives.
My thoughts remain with him,
for my shift goes on,
all hours of every day and every night.

Best Friend

For Dorit

We climbed the stairs in Montmartre,
we climbed to see the white basilica on its summit.
Standing on the glorious hill,
we watched the beauty of Paris.
History whispering tales,
charming streets,
that once were home to Monet, Picasso,
Dali, and Van Gogh.
We sat side by side
at the outdoor cafe,
watching people pass by.
We contemplated and discussed,
Dali's work,
that we had seen.
Sharing our thoughts on his genius and
his expression of the passage of time.
A couple sitting next to us,
shared a four-course meal,
a bottle of wine their companion.
We watched as they played with their food
and each other.
We giggled,
the way we did when we were young girls.
A dog took a whiz nearby
as we feasted on pasta and delicious bread.
Consumed by the moment we took a deep breath.
Space and time have not changed our friendship,
2 A.M phone calls,
emotional breakdowns,
life and loss,
we shared it all.
An ocean apart,
holding each other's hand through life.

Struggle

Walk a thousand miles
to learn a lesson,
not seeking perfection,
but seeking to be more human.
Pebbles on the road,
trials and tribulations along the way,
a life well lived.
I wish I could see the world
through your eyes.
I want to feel your beating heart,
when you feel fragile,
when you feel exposed,
when I hear your voice tremble with doubt.
The wind will whisper in your ear,
your inner compass will guide you.
If you stand in the rain,
and embrace the storm,
the struggle will bring tranquility,
strength
and wisdom.

Frozen

The delicious smells escaped the restaurant,
floating away.
I stood in the alley watching my son practicing
his Kung Fu forms,
while ducks roamed outside,
searching for food in the grass.
A storm of emotions was brewing within,
frozen I could not step through the double wood doors.
I could not breathe,
I could not walk into the past.
Dad loved the big round table,
the white tablecloth stiff with starch,
conversation would flow over
sweet and spicy bold flavors.
Dad would pour tea in the small ceramic cup
and delight in the moment.
He loved abundance of food,
and life
something he learned
while being hungry during the war.
He lived a big life,
and he knew the meaning of it.
I waited and waited,
building courage.
One day I conquered my fears,
and I walked through those doors,
like dipping my feet in the cold ocean,
small steps.
I walked in to pick up
take out,
love in small boxes of white and red.
Familiar faces were absent,
I sighed with relief.

I could not bear to tell the owner,
that I was alone,
that my parents are gone,
that I could never sit at the big round table again.
I took my boxes home,
closed my eyes,
and as I tasted the food,
 I remembered.

Your Footprints on My Soul

I clear the table,
traces of sunny side eggs,
red tomatoes, crumbs of whole wheat bread
and cappuccino in his new Father's Day mug.
I am an orphan
I say,
and he looks at me sideways.
orphans are small children, you are a grown woman.
In my heart lives a child
that no longer
has reaching arms to surrender to.
In my soul lives a child
that longs for the look in my father's eyes,
telling me that I am the sun and his stars.
I had wished this year would be easier,
lighter to carry
but the pain never leaves,
it saturates my dreams.
I celebrate the memory,
I celebrate life,
but today this grateful heart
remembers the footprints he left
forever on my soul.

A Home

For Irina and Josh

The walls bare,
waiting like a canvas to be painted
with your colors.
Missing pieces to a chest of drawers,
waiting for the internet connection,
sleeping on the air mattress on the floor.
Small details you share
through our conversation on the phone.
Your voice tired,
your voice eager,
building furniture for your new life.
"My girl and I are moving,"
I heard you say and I smiled,
because it sounded so sweet to me.
One thousand four hundred and seventy-five miles away,
bittersweet to watch you go,
holding my breath in anticipation.
Decorate your home with laughter that you share,
fill your home with the love you make,
moments that build your life.
Inspire one another
and find sanctuary in each other's arms.

Fifth Grade Graduation

I heard people say that you have big shoes to fill,
to follow your brother's footsteps.
Son, you are making your own mark,
your own footprints.
Your eyes shine with knowledge and wisdom of an old soul.
Words map your world,
destinations you have yet to conquer.
You follow your vast imagination.
Daily stories,
magical secrets of fifth grade,
that you share with me while we
read side by side.
I soak in details of your world.
As a toddler, you had imaginary friends,
at school, you created real friendships.
Trails of sand from the playground
followed you home.
Tin foil dinosaurs you brought
to life with your words.
Greek mythology and paper airplanes,
monsters in Minecraft.
Giant brown eyes filled with endless compassion.
Dream your big dreams,
embrace the world with both arms.
Lend a hand to someone in need,
listen to your heart.
If storms come your way,
find the sunshine within you.
Struggle will only make you stronger.
Reach for mountain peaks,
live with wonder in your heart,
but most of all find the joy in everything.

Mountains

The water rolls off my fingers,
as I wash the raspberries,
the same way your words roll off your tongue.
The raspberries bleed, my heart bleeds.
Sweating the small stuff,
invades our world .
Life is short I always say,
through the tears I see
that if I moved mountains for you,
it would not be enough.

Life

Love bugs on my car,
holding on while the rain comes down.
Peridot fields stretch for miles,
on the road cows with colors like mosaic patterns.
My thoughts dancing,
thoughts of yesterday,
hopes for tomorrow.
The sound of your voice,
the sound of your laughter,
open the gates to my soul.
I have waited all my life for you.
We grew together,
like seeds,
side by side,
arms outstretched,
soul to soul.
You became a man
with purpose and resolve.
I raised you,
days swiftly turning into years,
ordinary and extraordinary moments.
Your new life awaits,
I have to let you go,
so you can dream,
so you can be.
My heart trembles,
I wait on the sidelines,
I wait to see your face one more time.
When I'm gone,
you will remember.
You will remember the love
that I fed you,
the love that made you grow.

My Love

The pigeons ate seeds and bread crumbs
in Trafalgar Square.
We left a trail behind,
while bronze lions
stood witness and guarded us,
as I sheltered you from the storms in our life.
Nelson's statue overlooking the square winked at me,
I watched him with admiration.
Life is not a rehearsal grandma said,
we took in the moment as we inhaled our breath.
I stood in a dark place,
unwilling to surrender.
Fearless when it came to me,
afraid when it came to you.
London poetic in spirit,
as we listened with our hearts,
wide and open.
I wanted to live for you, my child.
Move the earth and the clouds for you.
Heal you with love,
lift you with laughter.
I hope that you remember
for the journey was long ago,
but I carry it all in my heart.

My Faith

His margins are clear,
while mine are complicated.
I carry faith in the pocket of my heart,
somewhere between the chambers
and the walls.
He is black and white,
while I am pink and grey.
My margins may be complicated,
but I live my truth,
clear,
organic,
loud.

Jerusalem
St. James

The ancient city knows my name.
Once this land was home.
I laid at her feet,
touched her,
listened to her heartbeat from the ground.
When I was small I hopscotched under her glorious beauty
while she winked at me.
That was long ago,
I return to heartbreak.
I skip through Jerusalem,
her eyes dark and tender as they follow me.
I search through her curves
to find his church,
nestled away, standing humble.
I enter the gates,
embraced by the sound of chanting,
rising through locked doors.
The doors open and I walk in
slowly feeling the spirit as the sunlight
enters through the vaulted dome.
My hearts skips a beat,
wishing my love was here,
to taste this moment.
The smell of incense
floating in the air,
awakens my senses,
as I sit in silence,
breathing it in for him,
breathing it in for me.

The One for Me

You live,
you love,
with passion in your veins.
A man with a boy's heart,
you delight in hermit crabs,
and finding a school of bait.
You cast a net like a matador,
in a bullfight.
Your arms strong,
your lines flowing.
I love the fire in your eyes,
those eyes know me,
the way they know the tides.
Your hands know me,
the way they know a tug of a Marlin or a shark.
When the Marlin dances,
there is wonder in your eyes.
The way your eyes shine
when I wrap myself around you
and melt into you.
You live,
you love,
you create art and beauty
from the moments of our life.

Rachel's Story Holocaust

The snow never melted that winter,
it didn't fall like powder.
It was harsh and unforgiving,
the way the days were,
grey and dark.
Death was a companion,
stench was in the air.
They were left to freeze and die.
The train transported them like cattle.
The train brought them here to perish.
Their lives left behind,
home, a faint warm memory.
Five-year-old Rachel, sat by the window,
she wondered if God had abandoned them.
She could not understand
the emptiness growing within,
the silent desperation screaming.
She heard of others that came with them
on the train,
freezing to death.
Their clothes traded for a bowl of food,
to survive another day,
to watch another sunrise.
The days bleak,
endless,
bitter cold.
Rachel watched from the small window,
every day a carriage
of dead bodies pass her by.
She didn't cry,
her heart was broken,
her mind was racing.
Memories that she would carry
all her life.

Her Needlepoint

Brother,
life is a journey,
that took us through storms,
and tangled woods,
and dark places.
Remember our home,
warm and loving.
We built forts
out of pillows and bedsheets.
We pretended to be cowboys,
like the ones we watched in the local theater.
Italian western films with subtitles,
starring Giuliano Gemma.
I remember his full lips
and dark eyes that drew me in.
I was the tag-along baby sister,
that you dragged with you,
as you voiced your protest on deaf ears.
My eyes wide open,
to your mischief,
flirtations with girls
and trash talk with your friends,
attempting to keep your secrets.
A cigarette you used as a bribe,
to keep my mouth shut.
You explained french kissing to me at seven,
since I overheard you with your friends.
You lured me into playing cards,
and you won my allowance,
until I got wise.
Simple days,
childhood memories,
a lifetime ,
we have shared.

As we laid mom to rest next to dad,
we shared tears,
our heartbreak would leave scars on our soul.
Home, far away,
across the ocean.
Memories that will remain,
in our hearts,
in our veins,
in the canvas of the needlepoint,
mom stitched called life.

Valentine

I taste the ocean on your lips
as you devour mine.
The wind sings her song,
and runs her fingers through your hair,
but your heart belongs to me.
The waves lull you to sleep,
but you seek the fire in my eyes.
You find life in my desire,
as my heart melts in your hand.
A love note by the bed,
a single rose on the kitchen table,
knowing glances,
melted dark chocolate in a bowl,
a dance through our life.
You read me like a book,
inhaling my pages,
light and dark,
taking them in as your breath.
You carried me through sadness,
through emerald green fields,
through aquamarine waters.
Valentine's Day, every day.
Hard to remember,
that life is fragile,
only this moment promised.
Not always roses or sunshine,
not always picture perfect,
sweet and sour,
sane and insane,
but always true,
always me and you.

Never Said Goodbye

For Grandma Ginca

She held my heart,
and lifted it to the heavens with
her love.
She died in a foreign land,
all alone.
She could not hear my cries,
she could not feel my embrace.
I was a child,
that carried my grief deep inside.
In my dreams she comes,
glorious as the ocean,
bright as the sun.
When I awaken she is gone.
I can't remember the sound of her voice,
all I remember is her loving smile.
I want to remember the smell of her hair,
I want to remember the softness.
I wish I was there when she died,
I wish I could make her resting place
as beautiful as she was.
I wish I could scatter flowers every day,
so her spirit can dance.
She is far away,
in a distant land,
but in my dreams she comes,
glorious as the ocean,
bright as the sun.

Daisy and Her Boy

Her boy comes home,
she greets him at the door.
Her tail wags as she follows him
down the hallway.
He's been to Boston,
Pittsburgh,
he's been to Washington D.C.
and Dallas.
She can smell the cities scents on his luggage,
of faraway places she had never been to.
She lies down sprawled
by his bed,
and moans with delight as he scratches
her ears with love.
In the kitchen, mom is cooking,
sounds of meat seared,
potatoes added,
cumin and garlic,
his favorite.
The dish a feast to the eyes,
Carmel colors bleed unto the plate.
The boy talks about the sick people he wants to help,
medical missions,
and things that are foreign to her.
She listens to the conversations,
decisions are to be made
about places he will go to live.
On his quilt,
she inhales the scent of his pillow,
while she watches them come and go.
She doesn't hunt for a trail of crumbs,
or Milk Bone cookies.
Her yellow fur is turning white,
she wags her tail with gratitude.

She is no longer a puppy,
and he is a grown man.
At the moment her boy is back
and that is all that matters.

A Slow Death

The mask covers her face,
creasing her beauty,
unforgiving.
Oxygen hissing like a venomous snake,
my brain in a bubble of doubt,
questioning life and death,
questioning everything.
Crackle sounds,
she is drowning
and I can't save her.
A life preserver nowhere in sight.
I feel it on my skin,
I feel it deep in my being.
There is no beauty to
how she hangs on to life
on a frayed string.
The sun enters
but I hide in the shadow,
I don't want the sun to watch me weep.
She melts into the bed,
and I wonder if she is dreaming of her
life and love.
I want her to stand on the shore
and wave goodbye.
I don't want her to struggle
as she drowns.
I come undone,
with every sound,
with every moment.
I come undone
as I watch her die.

A Humble Hero

For Grandpa Nathan

The kitchen is flooded with light.
Sun dancing on the walls.
I hear familiar footsteps,
and his sweet voice,
"mama when I grow up,
can you give me the recipe for chicken cutlets."
My son's face eager,
his eyes brilliant.
My mind drifts,
my voice trails,
"it's not just a recipe, it's about love,"
I answer.
Memories of my grandfather,
a tower of strength,
an inspiration.
In the ghetto he cooked,
he smuggled food,
he saved lives.
Sharing what little he had with others,
so they can survive the disease and hunger.
My grandfather was caught,
beaten,
thrown down into a ravine.
He was left to die
but he didn't.
He never spoke of his pain,
he carried it within.
He survived the war,
a hero humble and true.
Years later in his sunlit restaurant kitchen,
he stood,
varicose veins mapped his legs.

Large hands pounding chicken cutlets,
his strength towering,
not missing a beat.
Cooking with love was his life.
At times on sunny days, he seemed grey and
I wondered if the sounds and smells seeped back in.
I wondered if the echoes remained.
In this moment I look at my son
and I smile,
"it's not the recipe, it's about the love."
Little boy with veins rich with legacies,
filled with pain and courage,
rich with survival of the human spirit.
Generations linked,
legacies left,
love passed through time.

The Pain Never Leaves

If I uncover my pain,
will you soothe my soul?
If I show you my scars,
will you touch them?
Will you join me
down the brick wall corridor,
colored with despair.
The smell of stale air
and urine floated through the walls.
A grey-haired woman
held a doll while she wept,
clutching it for dear life,
repeatedly voicing her fear,
"it's mine."
Her eyes glazed seeking redemption,
seeking what she has lost.
The elevator with a code
to enter and to leave.
The corridor like a highway of lost souls,
and broken dreams.
A woman wearing ripped clothes,
licking her fingers,
ice cream covered her face like a blanket.
My brain was numb,
my heart was pounding,
I did not want to leave mom there.
I planned an escape,
I wanted to lift her
on my shoulders,
and carry her home,
where she belonged.
I did not recognize her.
I was scared for her,
I was scared for me.

I could no longer breathe.
They claimed that she will walk again,
in this rehab hell hole.
They claimed that she would mend.
I wanted her to walk,
I wanted her to fly.
The cries I heard were mine,
as I shattered inside into a million pieces.
I became a shadow of myself,
with fractured pieces of my soul.

A Potato in His Pocket

For Grandpa Antranik

The grey-haired man walked,
a potato tucked safely in his pocket.
The past was his constant companion,
his heart longed for his homeland.
The tapestry of his life woven
by threads of pain and strength.
The grey-haired man,
was once a boy that lived across the ocean,
persecuted for his religion.
His mother was murdered,
left bleeding by her infant son.
The infant grew into a brave boy,
he saved a train of children destined to die.
He jumped off the train,
and pleaded with the American soldiers,
to listen to his plight.
His picture was published
in the newspaper.
A hero,
the boy wearing only a tattered men's dress shirt.
The boy with dark bright eyes,
he ran like the wind,
with the will to survive.
His voice rose with courage,
his determination,
brought salvation
to all those children that day.
The grey-haired man,
never quite forgot,
the taste of grass he ate from the ground,
escaping to the mountains to stay alive.

He never forgot the hunger,
the potato in his pocket tucked away,
the potato in his pocket a source of comfort.
The past his companion,
all the days of his life.

Rose Jelly Made by Rose

For Grandma Rose

The glass jar clear and fragile,
like memories contained of yesterday.
Roadside wild roses awaited her,
on the way to Shinnecock Bay.
Dark red petals with intoxicating scent.
Her spirit joyous, her hands gentle,
she made jelly sweet with love.
Grandma's hands,
grandma's voice,
grandma's grace.
The glass vessel clear and fragile,
summer recollections whisper of framed snapshots.
Hidden away in a dark cupboard,
twenty-one years she's been gone,
yet the glass jar remains sealed,
saved memories,
timeless,
honored and cherished.

The Game of Life

Dust settled on the chessboard,
the queen and king no longer dance,
through the square green patches on the board.
The gardens are silent with sadness.
The little boy waited for them to awaken
and play hide and seek with the knight and the bishop.
He dreamt,
his mentor gone.
He remembered the wisdom taught,
the lessons of defeat ,
and the triumph of victory.
His grandpa's wisdom,
about the art of living.
His instruction of the game,
his kindness.
The boy became a man,
as he reached for the stars,
as he jumped over the hurdles of life,
he whispered under his breath,
"checkmate! This one is for you grandpa."

The Starfish Graveyard

Sweltering summer day,
sweat beads dancing on my skin.
We enter a starfish graveyard,
at the Key West souvenir shop.
I hear the ocean moaning,
whispering with regret,
whispering of loss.
On the ocean floor they frolicked,
on the ocean floor they lived.
Long ago,
my love gave me a red and orange starfish,
from the ocean floor.
We gazed at it with wonder,
and we set it free.
I hear the ocean mourning,
and I mourn the life and death,
the beginning and the end,
of all living things.

Fontainebleau

She is the jewel of Miami Beach,
she stretches like Sunday morning.
Her glory in her navel,
she dazzles as her gems
adorn her.
Saturday night,
short skirt wearing,
high heels Jimmy Choo,
cookie cutter crowds,
desire to enter her womb.
Desire to lay in her inviting arms,
as she sighs.
Her crescent shape seen Elvis and Sinatra,
she held their secrets as she whispered in their ears.
Over time she has grown more beautiful,
I remember her when we were young.
I remember a gentler time,
when the wine lasted,
through the night.
As we waited for tomorrow to be ours,
we watched the world go by.

To Be Human
Paris

Umbrellas zigzag through
the rain.
The beauty of these Paris avenues not lost on us.
She says,
"I feel like a herd of cattle."
I laugh as I take it all in,
"I feel like a butterfly."
We walk in and out
of museums
filled with wonder,
trying to breathe in some humanity,
into our veins.
As we inhale the timeless art,
drops of our spirit,
seep back into our core.

I Eat Seeds

"Who eats seeds, " he asks.
"Birds?" he questions.
As I hold the bag,
his eyes watching me.
I want to say that maybe I was a bird
in another life,
and that is why I love the sky and the ocean.
I smile,
because if I was a bird,
I could fly over rooftops,
resting on windowsills while
watching the world go by,
nature's reality television.
" I eat seeds," I answer.
I hold the sunflower seed bag proudly,
still smiling.
I drift away,
to the past,
I was eight,
holding mom's hand
in a noisy street in Tel-Aviv.
At a shop full of barrels,
filled with seeds and nuts,
and dried fruit.
The aroma of pistachio and almond intoxicating.
Armed with the bag of savory delights,
we would head on home.
Friday night,
I would soak in
the conversations,
on books, politics, and life's wisdom.
As I listened to dad and friends,
I would taste the seeds,
I would taste life.

A Corner in the World

At the age of two he knew,
life was not perfect.
We entered our new house,
the smell of fresh paint,
held us in a cloud.
I watched him moving
his fort and his soldiers,
his face beamed.
This was our corner of the world,
the nightmares would not seep through, these walls.
I would not let them enter.
For years I held secrets,
in a bottomless purse that I carried.
As he grew,
he scattered them,
as if they were seeds,
allowing them to be free.
As the bubbles came up from the deep,
we rose above,
and we began to breathe.

Wisdom

Life is the tapestry we weave.
Our journey filled with lessons learned.
We scatter seeds of knowledge retrieved,
passing them lovingly to our children.
Teaching them to break the chains,
of generations that came before them.
We love them so they can,
We guide them so they will,
rise above the ordinary and seek,
and embrace the challenge calling their name.

Holocaust Remembrance Day

They lit torches,
names were read in
observance of those gone.
Cries are rising from the earth,
ashes scattered,
fragments of humanity.
Sixty-six years since the liberation
of Auschwitz-Birkenau,
Sixty-six years since other liberation's,
the pain throbs,
of unspeakable truths.
You asked me to never forget,
those days of your life,
your childhood robbed,
your faith shattered.
Today I remember,
the lives lost,
the lives saved.
Today I remember those silent,
and those that chose to help.
I remember
you rising above the pain,
to survive,
to thrive, to live, to love.

Summer

You dove into the ocean,
and gave me a starfish,
red and orange and full of life.
I marveled at how beautiful it was.
I set it free,
the way I unchained the past.
Your eyes sparkled,
like the stars that
mapped our way home
my laughter,
was the music in the
warm summer night.

How Did He Survive?

How did he survive?
He watched his rabbi hanging,
with his tongue severed.
He watched a mass graveyard of bodies,
the stench filled the air,
the stench filled his senses.
How did he survive?
This black and white world,
where death came uninvited.
Sorrow was the background of his childhood,
dreadful clouds over the ghetto.
He was only a child,
I wonder how he survived.
I wonder how he didn't lose his mind,
this pain throbbing in his heart.
When I think of him,
and hold him in my dreams,
I wonder of these many things.
His road filled with pain,
became a road of endurance,
a road of triumph.

The Tango

Last night you tangoed with me,
around the room,
drawing me into your arms.
Today you tango with a Marlin,
luring him into your line.
He shakes his head in defiance,
you are the matador,
and he is the bull.
He does not surrender,
it's all a dance in this thing we call life.
You touch him,
he does not heed.
You feel the majesty of
your encounter.
Your soul soaring,
with gratitude
as you let him back into the ocean.
His safe release both his happiness, and yours.

His Lover

The ocean is his lover,
his skin tastes of her saltiness,
her scent lingers in his hair.
When she is fierce and unforgiving,
he finds his way back home to me,
and I kiss his inner tears.
I cradle him the way she does.
When he hears her whisper his name,
he listens,
and he surrenders,
willingly.
When he is old,
he wants to lay beside her.
As he dips in her blue waters,
she will soothe his soul,
and he will soothe mine.

I Thought I Might—I Still Do

As a young girl I thought,
that I might change the world.
I was fueled with desire and passion to try.
Second Avenue was barely lit up,
cardboard was sprawled on the sidewalk.
The shelter closed down the doors,
the streets were dark and dangerous.
My cooler filled with milk containers,
brown paper bags with homemade sandwiches,
that I handed out to strangers.
They welcomed me with silent gratitude.
My thoughts were dancing in my head,
I wanted to change their world.
I thought I should and could.
I thought I might someday.
There's a tree in my soul,
its branches are adorned with leaves,
its roots are tangled and twisted.
The past chains me with shackles,
social change has been too slow.
As a young girl I thought that I could change the world,
a part of me still believes.

The Novelty of a Ball

He was a thirteen-year-old boy,
war was cruel, sad, and gray.
There was no place to escape,
there were dreadful, piercing, loud sounds.
There was gratitude to be alive.
A ball made out of rags,
such a novelty in that place.
The stench of death always looming.
The boy grew up to survive,
the camp, the war, the sadness.
The boy was my dear father,
not only he survived the war,
but his spirit always soared high.
He lived his life with gratitude.
Growing up he was my hero,
he taught me by his example.
To fight for what I believe,
to live on my own terms.
To be kind and help others,
to seek truth and live fully.
His life read like a novel,
his legacy continues through our life.

Daniel—The Early Years

You tell me tales
about your day.
You tell me tales about
the trail of sand in your shoes.
You tell me tales about fossils
that you excavate in the schoolyard.
You are so proud
of the treasures that you find,
coconut leaves,
and rocks.
You tell me tales
about the games
that you invent,
and about a shark
that you drew.
I listen to your tales
amazed by every story
that you divulge.
I listen to your tales
happy to be the keeper of your secrets.
I listen and treasure your stories
the way I treasure you.

This Is All We Have

The divine exists in the details,
in the mornings,
in the tangerine sunrise.
If we lay our lips to it
we could taste life for a moment.
We could succumb to the truth,
that today is all we have.
The certainty that tomorrow
we will mourn today.
Today with all its
grace,
fear,
challenges,
humility,
and shame.
We must grasp it fiercely,
feel it in our marrow,
hold the vision of it in
the mantle of our minds.
This,
here and now,
is what we have.
It is not lost on me.
Watch my bright eyes,
wild with anticipation.
See the nectar roll off my chin,
listen to me roar loudly,
and know that
I am aware
that this is all we have to hold on to.

Israel

Her rivers flow through my veins.
Her mountains majestic in my dreams.
Her honey drips on my lips.
Her arms are outstretched to me.
Her orange groves awaken
a yearning I had forgotten.
Her heartbeat pounding through
my day.
Her breath on my face
whispering lullabies of a land
possessed by splendor.
Her life spreading on my skin
like wildfire.
I trace my fingers through
her borders.
I kneel before her with anticipation
and trepidation,
consumed by her beauty and grace,
feeble with love,
whole again.

His Landscape
Aiden

His fingers play with
my jingle-jangle bracelets.
Wood beads from India,
Chinese coins my friends and I wear,
an eye encased in gold to ward
off evil spirits,
Buddha with a turquoise bead
and a ladybug.
He touches them gently
feeling each one,
knowing them the way
he knows my lullabies.
The way he knows my voice,
when we dream about the moon and the stars.
When I move away he stretches
to find me in his sleep,
to find the curve of my waist,
where I held his father long ago.
I listen to his breath,
his presence fills my soul.
I dream big dreams for him.
I build memories,
they echo the laughter we share.
A landscape he can remember
and carry in his heart,
the way I carry him in my being.

Fishing Is Life

For Garo, My Dear Father in Law

The stars followed you.
The sun kissed your lips.
The wind embraced you,
and the tides listened to you weep.
You lived the mysteries of life
with sacred awe,
to the drops of happiness and sorrow.
The words are constricted
in my heart.
We laughed and
we wept
by your bedside,
as you floated
through two worlds.
We reminisced of days
with life.
The life that wakes you up
and shakes you up
as you feel it in your marrow.
Days of endless ocean,
sea life,
love and pain.
Days when your lion heart
was wild with wonder,
fierce with quest.
You loved,
you lived,
your chalice always full,
your roar loud,
your brave heart gentle.

Without You

Your absence is loud.
It echos through my being,
it tears through my heart.
Ten years,
I have walked thousands of days
and nights without you
by my side.
How?
How have I navigated the storms
life presented?
How did I hold onto small things that
you would have seen large,
the way only you could see,
and feel my soul
through the sweet and sour.
Days,
months,
years.
You missed the constellations
in my boy's eyes,
the miracle of my grandson
with your middle name
and your smile.
I don't know how grief morphs through
months and years.
Then,
in an instant,
the change is aroused by
a sound,
a smell,
evoking memories of home.
I see you in my poetry,
in my brilliant boys,
in kindness within me.

A kindness I learned from you.
Your legacy is alive.
Your legacy is as big as
you will always be to me.

Roar

As long as I have truth,
I will walk in your shadow
with my palms open.
I will feed your soul
with raw seeds,
and crumbled dreams
of my bruised ego.
I will flood the chambers of
your heart
with light.
Learning will happen in spaces
of defeat and rage,
in a fine line of silence and roaring,
tuning the sounds of life and
digesting the
lessons that set us free.

Collision

Underneath this great life,
an earthquake is brewing,
a shifting of the plates
under our feet.
I sense it,
I can almost touch it.
How did we get here?
The collision
is sudden,
unannounced.
Words spill,
littering the highway of life.
We remember how it began,
unaware of how it ends.

Choice

Tend to your garden,
cultivate it,
or scorch it down with gasoline.
Heal the blisters on
your tongue,
revive the beauty rooted
in love.
Stand in the dark
or claw your way
toward the light.
It's your choice
to live
or die.

Shadows

Stories are written in the margins
of life,
on broken wings,
on calloused fingers.
Love breathes oxygen there.
Life exists
where black and white
transform into hues of grey.
Where dreams are tasted
but not lived.
Truth is questioned,
loyalty is tested,
shadows grow wings
abandoning the darkness behind.

Spring

My hungry heart
whimpers like a dog
that wants to stay out of the rain.
My hungry heart
awakens
to the shades of green in the grass
and the blue of the sky,
breathtakingly limitless.
The senses sharper
with the birth of spring.
The smell of life new.
Empty holes, filled with
beauty and sorrow,
with blessings and loss,
overtake the moment.
Untouched
but seen.
Seen
and felt
underneath our skin.

March for Our Lives

For Parkland

Let truth enter the light of day,
as the sun rises so will our voices.
Let truth stir our souls,
swim through our marrow,
rise through our chants.
"Am I next?"
asks a little one
holding a sign,
his wispy curls cover his face.
We march,
we chant,
our voices boisterous,
demanding change.
The streets transformed
into a sea of humanity.
This moment rings with
the truth of stolen innocence,
of fear and fury,
of memories of those
taken too soon.
Thoughts and prayers
no longer welcome.
"Enough is enough,"
we plead.
Silence replaced by conversation.
Demands urged to be met by action.
This moment
awakens a fire
within our souls.
The tide has changed,
we stand
shoulder to shoulder.

The noble fight begins in unity.
One voice,
one vision,
one dream.

My Angel

The morning after Halloween,
the leaves were scattered
on the ground,
the air was crisp,
the sky was a glorious blue.
I caught a glimpse
of Bella,
my heart stopped for a moment,
my thoughts caught up .
The beautiful Shorthaired Pointer,
walked with grace,
intention,
and beauty.
My heart longed for
you, Angel.
Your brown eyes filled with
promise and pure love.
Your floppy ears swung
as you chased lizards and butterflies.
You ran in the fields,
you danced,
you looked for the light in our eyes
and you listened to our tender words.
You swam on endless summer days,
the sound of cicadas in the air,
you watched the fish swim by.
Our hearts full of your memory and
the life we shared.
Forever you will be remembered
and loved.

Our dear German Shorthaired Pointer passed away on February 2010.
She was an amazing dog and a part of our family. I wrote this poem
after seeing *Bella*, a neighborhood dog. Every time I see her my heart
skips a beat.

I Am Enough

The light does not wish to be the
darkness.
The Finch does not wish to be
an Eagle.
The thorn does not ask to
be the rose.
The sunrise does not wish to be
the sunset.
The lake does not wish to be
an ocean.
The sun does not wish to be the
moon.
Neither do I wish to be anyone
but
myself.

The Beauty That Is Life

The leaf bathes
in the morning light,
floating with grace and beauty.
The geese
welcomed new life today.
The trees whispered
of spring as I walked by.
At dawn I listened
to him breathing.
The moment magnified
by its simplicity,
by the truth
of the beauty that is life.
He is the one
the dog followed home,
he kept him and made him his own,
protected and loved him
to the end.
He is the son that held his mother
as she shook with chemo
and life.
He is the one
that delights in a screeching reel
and the cat that follows him to the lake.
He is the one that feeds the squirrels
and thinks to buy a cup of joe
for the crossing guard.
He is the one with fire
in his veins.
He is the one that holds me
when the day is dark
and the night is empty.
He looks into my eyes
and sees my soul.
He is the one.

The Cup

He drank Turkish coffee
from the Meissen cup.
His testament to impermanence,
his gratitude to survival.
The walls of the room
a colorful canvas
a celebration of art.
The cup,
hand painted a hundred years ago
was delicate, rare, and beautiful.
He drank the coffee slowly,
savoring the darkness
mixed with the sweetness.
He drank slowly
the way he lived his life with purpose.

The Salvation That Is Yoga

The dark room is
filled with light,
filled with energy,
moving through the room.
The fly on the wall,
watches us as we move in unison.
As we reach an inner peace,
filled with gratitude to the universe.
Our instructor spreading seeds of knowledge,
words of letting go,
words of connections to one another.
Letting the ego dance outside our bodies.
The knowledge that we are perfect as we are,
the love of acceptance.
She scatters the seeds,
and we collect them,
our spirit blooms,
a ray of sunshine follows us home.

Fifty-Seven

My interior life is complete.
Boys that reside in my soul,
words that I breathe,
as I contemplate,
the state of duality of life.
My interior life is complete,
with mindfulness,
with each inhaling breath
guiding me to the light,
guiding me to inner peace.

Depression

Summer in its glory
is almost over,
and I have not gone to the island,
not once,
to stretch in the water,
to watch the jellyfish at my feet.
I long to lay in the crystal blue waters
and to feel alive.
The seagulls are calling,
the Pelicans too,
they want to know where I have been.
They can't imagine that I've been sitting,
surrounded by four walls,
anchoring down,
writing half poems,
and watching geese and owls in
my morning walks.
I long for the water
to wash over me,
to awaken my soul.

Solitude

My heart trembles,
my heart floods,
underneath the malnourished past.
Memory breathes life
into the body,
memory shakes it from its slumber.
Awakened to the touch
ever so softly,
like a whisper on the skin,
like feathers in the wind.
Love seared into the being,
buried in a cavern of yesterday
where fragile and tenderness
once lived.
Famine and solitude
were a choice in
a narrative of a crumbling world.
Denial and deprivation were a choice.
Love came breathing life back into me,
slowly,
gently,
setting me free.

Sunday Morning
Aiden

Sunday,
thunder pierced the morning.
You fell asleep,
your arms stretched above your head
in surrender
to your dreams.
Lions, giraffes in Africa,
tales I tell you about the sun and stars,
colorful starfish and majestic
blue marlin living in the ocean, as
you sank into your dreams.
You touched my face,
your nails on my skin,
happiness climbed to meet you,
like the new day.
Short breaths,
joyous sounds,
are things I hold as miracles,
for the love I feel is extraordinary.
Your eyelashes flutter,
evanescence, beauty
of the moment.
I cover your head with kisses,
my heart open to you,
and the universe.

My Beloved and the Wind

The light penetrated through the clouds,
I watched fireflies entangled in a dance.
The blue Jay jeered attempting
to distract me,
and the hawks.
The wind silently
caressed my face.
If tomorrow does not come
it will be enough.
If I don't lay in your arms once again
or roll in the sand with you,
it will be enough.
If tomorrow does not come,
and I don't touch the dew on the grass
at daybreak,
if I don't feel the edges of a book
cutting my skin and soul
as I linger and kiss your neck,
if tomorrow does not come
I would have had enough
because you had loved me.

Wondrous

I dove into the ocean
to catch a glimpse
of a sea turtle.
I saw him for a moment,
a flash.
Majestic,
grand,
my heart fluttered,
my spirit soared.
I saw pods of dolphins
in the wild,
leaping,
frolicking like children in
the playground,
and my heart rejoiced.
I saw wondrous things
without a plan nor a compass to lead the way.
Curiosity was my only guide
and my willingness to fail.

Going Home

Her rivers pulsate in the veins of my mind,
her desert's wilderness on my skin.
Her land a piece of my narrative,
she thunders in the echoes of my thoughts,
in the geography of my being.
The soundtrack of my childhood,
the backdrop of the present moment.
My roots tangled
with blurred lines,
of self,
of quest,
of devotion.